TOURISTS' PERCEPTIONS AND ASSESSMENTS

ADVANCES IN CULTURE, TOURISM AND HOSPITALITY RESEARCH

Series Editor: Arch G. Woodside

Recent Volumes:

ADVANCES IN CULTURE, TOURISM AND HOSPITALITY
RESEARCH   VOLUME 8

TOURISTS' PERCEPTIONS AND ASSESSMENTS

EDITED BY

ARCH G. WOODSIDE
Boston College, MA, USA

METIN KOZAK
Dokuz Eylul University, Izmir, Turkey

Emerald

United Kingdom − North America − Japan
India − Malaysia − China

Emerald Group Publishing Limited
Howard House, Wagon Lane, Bingley BD16 1WA, UK

First edition 2014

Copyright © 2014 Emerald Group Publishing Limited

Reprints and permission service
Contact: permissions@emeraldinsight.com

British Library Cataloguing in Publication Data
A catalogue record for this book is available from the British Library

ISBN: 978-1-78350-618-7
ISSN: 1871-3173 (Series)

Printed and bound by CPI Group (UK) Ltd, Croydon, CR0 4YY

ISOQAR certified
Management System,
awarded to Emerald
for adherence to
Environmental
standard
ISO 14001:2004.

Certificate Number 1985
ISO 14001

INVESTOR IN PEOPLE

CONTENTS

LIST OF CONTRIBUTORS

Maria D. Alvarez	Boğaziçi University, Istanbul, Turkey
Steve Brown	Flinders University, Adelaide, Australia
Chien-Fen Chiu	Arizona State University, Phoenix, AZ, USA
Hwansuk Chris Choi	University of Guelph, Guelph, Canada
Antónia Correia	CEFAGE, University of Algarve, Faro, Portugal
Giacomo Del Chiappa	University of Sassari, Sassari, Italy
Eyal Ert	The Hebrew University of Jerusalem, Rehovot, Israel
Juergen Gnoth	University of Otago, Dunedin, New Zealand
Burçin Hatipoğlu	Boğaziçi University, Istanbul, Turkey
Mariem Kamoun	University of Tunis, Tunis, Tunisia
Sangkyun Kim	Flinders University, Adelaide, Australia
Metin Kozak	Dokuz Eylul University, Foca, Izmir, Turkey
Woojin Lee	Arizona State University, Phoenix, AZ, USA
Rodrigo Murillo	Bradford School of Management, Bradford, UK
Steven Pike	Queensland University of Technology, Brisbane, Australia
Girish Prayag	University of Canterbury, Christchurch, New Zealand

Nik Alia Wan Ab Rahman	Flinders University, Adelaide, Australia
Helena Reis	University of Algarve, Faro, Portugal
Hamida Skandrani	University of Tunis, Tunis, Tunisia
HeeKyung Sung	Arizona State University, Phoenix, AZ, USA
Arch G. Woodside	Boston College, Chestnut Hill, MA, USA
Andreas H. Zins	MODUL University Vienna, Vienna, Austria

CHAPTER 1

PRIMER TO TOURISTS' PERCEPTIONS AND ASSESSMENTS INCLUDING HOW-TO-BUILD FORMAL, IMPLEMENTABLE, MODELS OF THE TOURIST GAZE

Arch G. Woodside and Metin Kozak

ABSTRACT

This primer defines and describes conscious and nonconscious perception and assessment processes by tourists. The primer links the field of tourism perception studies to the literature of experimental social psychology. The primer describes the important roles that metaphors play in connecting conscious and nonconscious thinking and how both tourism brand managers and tourists use metaphors to use stories to enable enactments and favorable outcomes of archetypal motivations. The primer introduces formal implementable models of the major tenet in Urry's tourist gaze − visitors' home culture automatically and mostly nonconsciously profoundly influences their perceptions, assessments, and interpretations of what they see when traveling and visiting away destinations. Model implementation includes applying Boolean

Tourists' Perceptions and Assessments
Advances in Culture, Tourism and Hospitality Research, Volume 8, 1−22
Copyright © 2014 by Emerald Group Publishing Limited
All rights of reproduction in any form reserved
ISSN: 1871-3173/doi:10.1108/S1871-317320140000008001

algebra-based asymmetric tests instead of symmetric matrix algebra-based statistical tests — the asymmetric tests examine for the consistency of high scores in perceiving, assessing, and behaviors of complex configurations of antecedent conditions. A detailed empirical example of asymmetric testing includes consistent high scores for Americans, Brits, Canadians, and Germans for not shopping for gifts to take home during their visits to Australia. This primer also introduces the concept of the tourist meta-gaze — seeing and assessing outside the automatically activated culturally based tourist gaze.

Keywords: Archetype; asymmetric; FMET; perception; meta-gaze; tourist gaze

INTRODUCTION: WHAT ARE PERCEPTIONS AND ASSESSMENTS?

While the two processes occur together usually and nearly simultaneously, distinguishing between perception and assessment is useful both for theoretical and practical reasons. "Perception" is directing attention to, interpreting, identifying, categorizing, naming, and frequently associating an object, living organism, process, or behavior with another object, living organism, process, or behavior. The perceptual steps — attending, interpreting, identifying, categorizing, naming — can, and usually do, occur automatically, nonconsciously, and with minimal effort (Bargh, 1982; Bargh & Chartrand, 1999; Bargh, Chen, & Burrows, 1996). Perceptions influence assessments and assessments influence perceptions; for example, unconsciously categorizing a trip/visit to "Disneyworld" to be a secular Mecca and symbol of middle-class membership influences the assessment by John and Mary Smith, living in Cleveland, Ohio, that taking their daughter, Judy (age 8), to be "the right, necessary, and good thing" to do. The place and membership category of Mecca and middle-class respectively, are unlikely to enter conscious awareness or verbal discussions by John and Mary. Judy is likely to be aware of Disneyworld and have some well-formed perceptions/understanding about what activities occur while visiting this location — when Judy was two-years-old she may have received a Mickey Mouse stuffed doll and has been watching the Disney TV channel ever since. Thus, all three, John, Mary, and Judy, attune automatically, interpret, identify, categorize, name, and associate (i.e., index) personally with the trope, "trip to

Disneyworld." Experiencing (e.g., watching the Disney channel) nurtures mental indexing (i.e., automatic unconsciously associating self with the object and behavior) (cf. Williams & Bargh, 2008).

"Assessment" is evaluating, rendering judgment, and frequently concluding with a valuation (e.g., "worth the money" and "not worth the time and effort"). Assessments can occur consciously and/or unconsciously though as a process, assessments occur mostly unconsciously (Zaltman, 2003; Zaltman & Zaltman, 2008). Conscious and unconscious expressions of attitude — both verbal and behavior — are expressions of assessments.

Metaphors Connect Conscious and Unconscious Perceptions and Assessments

Tourists, destinations, accommodation brands, attraction brands, travel-service brands (e.g., airlines), and researchers use metaphors to enable/ nurture both perceptions and assessments. A "metaphor" is a word, object, animal, place, or thing that expresses an association between two or more entities. The following statement expresses a metaphor, "If I was an animal, the animal that would be most likely is a rhinoceros." Here is another, "The animal that I would most want to become if I was an animal is an eagle." Researchers sometimes ask consumers metaphor-related questions to bring/verbalize unconscious thoughts into consciousness (Woodside, 2008, 2010). Consumers' use of metaphors connects to the archetypes that they seek unconsciously to enact (cf. Jung, 1916/1959, 2009) — archetype are primal forces that are ingrained innately to influence behaviors (Jung, 1916/1959; Wertime, 2002; Woodside, 2010).

Asking travelers to tell about themselves regarding the animal that they are most alike versus the animal they would most like-to-be is helpful for surfacing their perceptions and assessments about themselves and the brands having similar characteristics. Fig. 1 provides examples of research on consumer metaphor-indexing using this "forced-metaphor elicitation technique" (FMET). See Woodside (2008) for an elaboration of the FMET with examples from interviews with several additional consumers.

Fig. 2 is a visual metaphor that summarizes this introductory discussion. In Fig. 2 the two overlapping rounded-rectangles indicate high consistency of the association between perceptions and assessments. A total of nine distinct processing area appear with the unconscious association of P1A1 (perceptions•assessments) being the largest area in Fig. 2 — indicating P1A1 includes about half or so of the total processing efforts by humans.

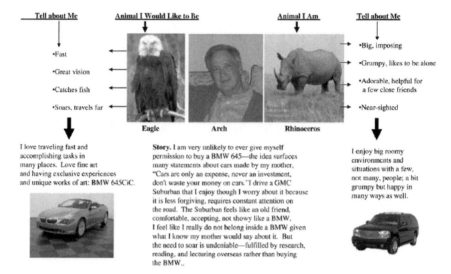

Fig. 1. Application of the Forced Metaphor Elicitation Technique (FMET). *Source*: Woodside (2008, p. 485).

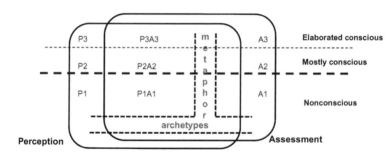

Fig. 2. Perception and Assessment of Contexts, Objects (Brands), Activities, and Outcomes. *Note:* P1, perception does occur sometimes without immediate assessment; P1A1, greatest amount of mental activity occurs here — nonconscious perception-assessment; P2, conscious awareness of perceiving; P2A2, mentally tuned into perceiving•assessing consciously; A2, consciously aware of assessing; P3, verbally describing perceptions; P3A3, verbal or formal (written) statements of perceptions•assessments; A3, verbal or formal (written) assessments. Metaphors are representations of emotions, beliefs, self, or others that express archetypal enactments. Archetype is a primal force that directs conscious and unconscious thinking and behavior innately.

The mid-level dot represents the "logical and" condition in Boolean algebra and the dot represents the union of both processes. Metaphors appear in Fig. 2 as a channel of natural occurrences that connect formal perceptions and assessments with archetypes. Collecting data that incorporates consumers' use of metaphors is helpful for opening-up, unlocking, consumers own-use of metaphors in their nonconscious perceptions•assessments processes (Woodside, 2008; Zaltman & Zaltman, 2008).

The dotted-lines for the vertical and horizontal respective channels for metaphors and archetypes are to indicate the porous nature of both. Both channels include bits and pieces of conscious and nonconscious thinking and elements of perception only, perceptions assessments, and assessment only thinking − once a metaphor or archetype appears mentally nonconscious and conscious thoughts can move into or out of the channels that aid or hinder the interpretation and assessment processes. The surfacing of an archetype via a metaphor does not guarantee that the typical story-ending of the metaphor is going to occur. Unconscious-to-conscious thinking about a trip to Disneyworld can result sometimes in negative assessments.

ISSUES THAT PERCEPTION AND ASSESSMENT ANSWER

In Fig. 2 formal perceptions include discussions with self and others focusing on answering questions such as, "What is it?" "How does it work?" "Who would do that?" "Who would want to buy that?" In Fig. 2 formal assessments include discussions with self and others focusing on answering such questions as, "Are we having fun yet?" "What are the benefits it (e.g., the destination, accommodation, attraction, and trip) offers" "What are the shortcomings from using it?" "Does it actually work well?"

Fig. 3 expands on Fig. 2 to emphasize that all human perceiving through a particular enculturated lens, that is, "One's eyes are socio-culturally framed and there are various 'ways of seeing'" (Urry & Larsen, 2011, p. 2). "There is no-thing 'out-there' intrinsically formed, interesting, good or beautiful as our dominant culture outlook would suggest. Vision is skilled cultural practice" (Jenks, 2004, p. 165). Urry and Larsen (2011) expand on Urry's (1992) prior contributions on the "tourist gaze":

> Humans gaze upon the world through a particular [a complex cultural configural] filter of ideas, skills, desires and expectations, framed by social class, gender, age, and

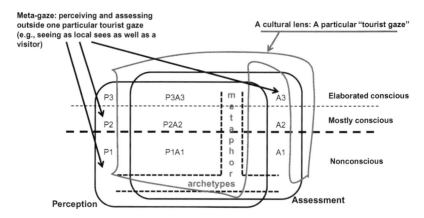

Fig. 3.　Perception and Assessment of Contexts, Objects (Brands), Activities, and Outcomes within a Tourist Gaze and Using a Meta-Gaze.

education. Gazing is a performance that orders, shapes, and classifies, rather than reflects the world. (Urry & Larsen, 2011, p. 2)

Thus, visitors to Australia from America, Canada, China, Germany, Korea, Russia, and Spain each are representative of different complex cultural configural gazes. These distinct configurations constitute unique tourist gazes that affect the perceptions and assessments of what members of each national culture see – and their behaviors while visiting Australia. Using Boolean algebra, models and research findings for the unique complex cultural configurations across nations support this observation (Hsu, Woodside, & Marshall, 2013; Woodside, Hsu, & Marshall, 2012).

Note in Fig. 3 that the example culturally derived tourist gaze does not encompass all of areas of perception and assessment. The possibility occurs for the tourist to interpret each of the nine regions of perception and assessment beyond her or his own cultural lens at least to a limited extent. This limited extent begins with the recognition that members of different cultures have different tourist gazes when viewing the supposedly same scene. Tourists' acculturation to see as locals and members of different cultures perceive and assess frequently begins with locals explaining the meanings that they assigned to in situ scenes and events as well as visitors becoming localized by adopting the language, customs, and gazes of members of a very different culture – a process that takes years to accomplish. The beginnings of such tourism acculturation processes can and do occur — Muziani (2006) reviews some this not-so-vast literature on attempting to "go native" and "looking local" by visitors to Southeast Asia.

A TOURIST GAZE IS A COMPLEX CONFIGURATION OF ANTECEDENT CONDITIONS EXPRESSING A SPECIFIC CULTURAL WAY OF VIEWING

Before Woodside, Hsu, and Marshall's (2011) examination of complex statements of culture configurations, the "net effects" individual dimensions in the tourist gaze was the focus of formal models of cultural influences on tourists' perceptions and assessments (e.g., MacKay & Fesenmaier, 2000; Pitts & Woodside, 1986). Well into the second decade of the 21st century, the dominant logic in tourism research is still to analyze cultural influences using positivistic tools that test for symmetric relationships (e.g., analysis of variance, multi-dimensional scaling, and multiple regression analysis, structural equation modeling). However, culture consists of complex configurations of antecedent conditions. Rather than study the impact of each dimension on perceptions, assessment, and behavior, Woodside et al. (2011) propose testing complex configurations of antecedents as entities using Boolean algebra. Such testing for asymmetric relationships examines whether or not a high scores for a complex antecedent condition associates with high scores for an outcome condition without testing whether or not low scores for the complex cultural statement associates with low scores on the outcome condition. Positivistic symmetric testing examines whether or not low scores for the antecedent associates with low scores for the outcome and high scores for the antecedent associate with high scores for the outcome.

Available, free, software (fsQCA.com) provides easy-to-apply tools for asymmetric testing of complex configurations (Ragin, 2008; Woodside, 2013). Fig. 4 shows examples of complex configurations of antecedent conditions using Hofstede's four principal cultural values as antecedents: individualism (I), power distance (P), uncertainty avoidance (U), and masculinity (M). The principal tenet of Hofstede's theory is that cultures vary by how much they display each of these four cultural values. For example, Japan is the nation with the highest country score for masculinity; the United States has the highest country score for individualism.

Considering only a high–low split on each of these four values, a total of 16 combinations are possible: high–low for each of the four values in

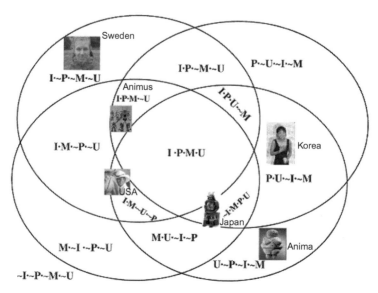

Fig. 4. Examples of Alternative Tourists' Gazes Applying Hofstede's Principal Values. *Note*: I, individualism; P, power distance; M, masculinity; U, uncertainty avoidance; "•", and; "~", not. Example: The complex configuration for the United States is high in individualism, high in masculinity, low in uncertainty avoidance, low in power distance (look for the cowboy with horse in the figure).

combination. For example, I•M•~U•~P represents the complex configuration of the four antecedent conditions for the United States, where the mid-level dot represents the logical "and" Boolean operation and the sideways tilde, "~", represents the negation of the condition. Thus, if the United States has the following (calibrated) values, I = .98; M = .75; ~U = .82; ~P = .64, the combination score equals .64. In Boolean algebra the value for the entire combination expression is equal to the lowest value for any single condition within the expression; such an operation expresses the amount of confluence (union) the given case (the United States is the case here) across the four values. For the complex statement, I•M•~U•~P, a score of .64 represents a high level of membership when computing the membership scores for each of the nations in the Hofstede (2001) data set.

Woodside et al. (2011) include findings from testing the impact of the following tourist gaze on tourists visiting Australia for not shopping for gifts to take home: the complex configuration of high individualism, high masculinity, and low power distance (I•M•~P). Fig. 5 summarizes some of

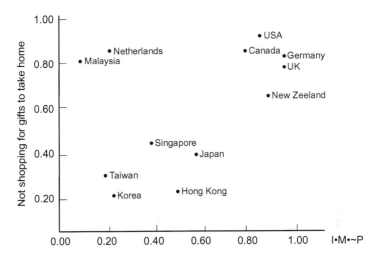

Fig. 5. How the Tourist Gaze of High Individualism, High Masculinity, and Low Power Distance (I•M•~P) Associates with Not-Shopping-for-Gifts among Visitors from Western Nations. *Source*: Woodside, Hsu, and Marshall (2011) describe these findings.

their findings. In asymmetric test, visitors from Canada, Germany, New Zeeland, and the United States have high scores for the complex antecedent condition and high scores in not shopping for gifts to take home. Visitors to Australia from Hong Kong, Korea, Japan, Malaysia, Netherlands, Singapore, and Taiwan have relatively low scores on I•M•~P. The findings that visitors from the Netherlands and Malaysia have high scores on not shopping for gifts as well has no effect on the conclusion about the high consistency (index) that a tourist gaze consistency of high I•M•~P has high levels of association in not shopping for gifts to take home. The tourist gazes for the Netherlands and Malaysia will consist of high scores on one or more other tourist gazes that associate with high not shopping for gifts.

Such findings for not gift shopping for gifts may not be particularly surprising for such a cultural configuration and tourist gaze of high individualism combined with high masculinity − individuals looking through such lenses are more likely to conclude that their visits are all about themselves and they have lower levels of concern about bringing back gift for family members and friends compared to a tourist gaze low individualism and low in masculinity (~I•~M). Also visitors from cultures low in power distance have lower need to display power through gift-giving in comparison to

visitors from nations high in power distance; thus, high scores in the complex configuration of I•M•~P associate with high scores in not shopping
for gifts.

The details of the findings (Woodside et al., 2011) regarding I•M•~P
and additional cultural configurations includes findings for young, middle-
aged, and older visitors to Australia for each of the originating countries.
Possibly unsurprising, the findings do not vary substantially across age segments. A distinct "youth culture" is more myth than fact – at least when it
comes to shopping for gifts to take home while visiting Australia.

PRACTICAL TOURISM MARKETING IMPLICATIONS FROM THE STUDY OF TOURISM PERCEPTIONS, ASSESSMENTS, AND THE TOURIST GAZE

Views through cultural lens describe the substantial impacts of the tourist
gaze on the success versus failure of tourism marketing campaigns. Two
examples illustrate this perspective. The following campaign theme to
attract Americans, Canadians, and British visitors to Australia was a huge
success – "I'll slip an extra shrimp on the Barbie [barbecue grill] for you,"
with the actual slogan of the TV commercials being "Come and say
G'day" – available for viewing at http://www.youtube.com/watch?v=Xn_
CPrCS8gs. Before the campaign launch in 1984, Australia was approximately number 78 on the "most desired" vacation destination list for
Americans, but became number 7 three months after the launch, and soon
became number 1 or 2 on Americans' "dream vacation" list, remaining in
that position for most of the next two decades (Baker & Peggy Bendel,
2005) – these findings do not represent a scientific true-experiment but are
useful practical indicators of success. The informal personal, low power distance, and masculine (a barbecue grill indicating masculine cooking and
spokesperson, Paul Hogan (later "Crocodile Dundee" in the movies)), indicating a guy's guy and a visual model high in individualism, masculinity,
and low in power distance (I•M•~P). Australia ran this campaign for so
many years that Paul Hogan threatened a law suit to end the campaign –
another indicator of high success.

So in 2006, with no reports on testing its impact on tourists' perceptions and assessments in American, British, or Canadian markets,
Australia launched a new TV campaign – "So where the bloody hell are
you?" (Available for viewing at http://www.youtube.com/watch?v = rn

0lwGk4u9o.) After spending $180 million (Australian dollars) the campaign was shut down in 2007. The commercial was initially banned by Broadcast Advertising Clearance Centre in the United Kingdom, which would not allow the word "bloody" in television versions of the commercial. Following lobbying by Tourism Australia, including a visit to the United Kingdom by Australia's tourism minister Fran Bailey and Lara Bingle, the ban was lifted, although a 9pm "watershed" was imposed on television commercials. In March 2007, the Advertising Standards Authority in the United Kingdom ordered the removal of roadside billboards bearing the slogan. The ASA stated that it had received 32 complaints and warned Tourism Australia to refrain from using profanity in future billboards. The Australian Tourism minister Fran Bailey responded, "What an absolutely, incredibly ludicrous stance and a greater example of double standards you'd never find. Everyone is shaking their heads, especially as it's in a country where they allow the FCUK billboards. ... I mean what is it about our campaign that they find offensive? I just don't understand it" (Brit ban, 2009). "After calling the ads 'great' at the time of their launch when he was in Opposition, Prime Minister Kevin Rudd subsequently stated: 'That campaign, every place I have visited in the world, has been basically described as an absolute rolled gold disaster'" (Wikipedia, 2014).

The advertisement has also been banned by regulators in Canada, owing to the implication of "unbranded alcohol consumption" by the opening line, "We've poured you a beer." There was also concern in Canada at the word "hell" being used as an expletive. It has been allowed to run with no adverse action in countries such as the United States and New Zealand. In Singapore, the advertisement campaign is presented as "So Where Are You?" with the words "bloody hell" removed (Wikipedia, 2014).

For Australia, heavy promotion of gift-buying for loved ones back home versus promoting enjoying experiences/events during your visit is likely to be an anathema to tourists gazing through a high I•M•~P cultural lens — their visits are particularly for their personal enjoyment — a time and place to pamper themselves. "So where the bloody hell are you!" TV commercial includes 11 visual vignettes/scenes from an Australian bar, camels, to the Sydney harbor, and a signature beach — multiple places and activities that match well with the pampering-oneself gaze of visitors from high I•M•~P cultures.

Yet, the bloody-hell message itself implies that the places and activities are insufficient to attract these visitors — unlike the "shrimp on the barbie" the bloody-hell you-are-missing message is the negation of an

invitation to visit and it is likely to cause difficulty in automatically assessing its actual intended appeal. These post hoc views could have been
confirmed or disconfirmed by pretesting the commercial in clutter by
showing the commercial in the middle of a run of 10 commercials for
various products and services with different commercial promoting visits
to Australia serving as a control commercial (see Woodside & Glenesk,
1984).

SOME BOOLEAN ALGEBRA EXAMPLES OF
ESTIMATING A TOURIST GAZE

This primer does not provide a full exposition of how to apply Boolean
algebra to test alternative complex configurations of scores on simple antecedent conditions. On an individual basis the simple antecedent conditions
can be used within recipes which include socioeconomic, demographic, and
cultural conditions or different combinations of these conditions. Consider
the simple and complex membership scores for the following four cases
(i.e., four tourists) for age, income, education, and culture:

- Case 1: Young (25), high-income (top 5%), medium educated (quintile 3)
  Japanese visitor
- Case 2: Older (68), high-income (top 5%), Japanese with high-formal
  education
- Case 3: Middle-aged (45), middle-income (quintile 3), highly educated
  (top 5%) American
- Case 4: Older (66), high-income (top 10%), moderately educated, Brit

For the complex configuration of age (A), income (I), education (E),
and Japanese culture (A•I•E•Japan), the complex antecedent-
configuration scores across the four cases are equal to 0.22, 0.57, 0.22,
and 0.18, respectively ((See Table 1) remember the complex membership

Table 1.

Case	Age	Income	Education	Culture: Japan (M•~I•U•P)	Culture: United States (M•I•~U•~P)
1	0.20	0.95	0.50	0.57	0.26
2	0.94	0.95	0.95	0.57	0.26
3	0.50	0.50	0.95	0.22	0.61
4	0.95	0.95	0.50	0.18	0.36

score is equal to the lowest membership score among the conditions appearing in the complex statement). Substituting the US culture into the equation (A•I•E•US), the membership scores for the four cases equal 0.26, 0.26, 0.22, 0.18, respectively. The calibrated culture membership scores for each of the four cultural values (M = masculinity; I = individualism; UK = uncertainty avoidance; P = power distance) for each culture (i.e., Japan and United States) were calculated by Hsu et al. (2013) and Woodside et al. (2011). Note the complex cultural score for a given country can be calculated for individuals from different cultures. Obviously Japanese visitors would score the highest, or close to the highest, for the complex configuration representing Japan (M•~I•U•P) and Americans would score highest, or close to the highest on the complex configuration representing the United States (M•I•~U•~P). The complex configuration for the British case has a relatively low score for the cultural configurations of the other two countries.

Using Hofstede (2001) calibrated index values, individuals (cases) from nearby or far-away countries may have close to the same calibrated membership scores on one or more simple cultural values and may or may not have similar membership scores for complex cultural configurations. Consider Americans' (US) and Canadians' (CAN) calibrated scores for masculinity: US = 0.60, CAN = 0.52; individualism: US = 1.00, CAN = 0.93; uncertainty avoidance: US = 0.31, CAN = 0.32; power distance: US = .34; CAN = .34. The complex configurations for these scores (M•I•~U•~P) for the two countries equal 0.60•1.00•0.69•0.66, thus, 0.60 for the US culture and 0.52•0.93•0.68•0.66, thus, 0.52 for the Canadian culture. Conclusion: using calibrated scores of Hofstede's original index value scores indicate that the Americans and Canadians have highly similar complex configuration scores − not a conclusion that most Canadians are likely to agree with. The take-away here is that the use of complex antecedent configurations of culture with or without additional socioeconomic and demographics built into the models are useful for building implementable models of the tourist gaze.

CONTRIBUTIONS TO TOURISTS' PERCEPTIONS AND ASSESSMENTS

This primer to tourists' perceptions and assessments includes the following brief introduction to each of the following 12 chapters in this volume. Each chapter offers a complex configuration of benefits from its reading. The chapters offer unique and valuable insights for advancing tourism theory and in planning effective tourism marketing practice by deepening the reader's understanding of tourists' perceptions and assessments.

You are asked in the following chapters to answer one or three questions for each chapter. Readers with 20+ correct answers are requested to inform Arch G. Woodside and Metin Kozak to receive a special HETPA Award − High Expertise in Tourist's Perceptions and Assessments. Be sure to include your mailing address and telephone number for the mailing of your award.

Nationality Differences in User-Generated Reviews in the Hospitality Industry

In Chapter 2, Maria D. Alvarez and Burçin Hatipoğlu describe individual evaluations of 40 Istanbul hotels by guests through an analysis of guest comments and hotel ratings posted in the Booking.com website. Questions for you to answer include the following items.

1. Who offers the most positive hotel assessments on average: French, United Arab Emirates, Germans, or Russians?
2. Who offers the most negative hotel assessments on average: French, United Arab Emirates, Germans, or Russians?

Circle your answers on this page before reading Chapter 2. If you answer correctly both times, add two points to your score for the total quiz.

Evaluation of the Service Performance: Applications of the Zone of Tolerance with Importance-Performance Analysis

In Chapter 3, Hwansuk Chris Choi, Woojin Lee, HeeKyung Sung, and Chien-Fen Chiu examine convention delegates' perceptions of product and service performance of a convention facility by applying IPA and ZOT. Utilizing the multiple-expectation standards, the ZOT-enabled technique allows researchers and practitioners to deepen understanding of customers' service expectations and to explore customers' tolerance levels toward each single service. This study shows that despite the fact that basic services have a narrower tolerance zone, respondents actually have the narrowest tolerance zone toward the performance services and have quite similar tolerance zones toward basic and excitement services. The study data were collected at the Phoenix Convention Center (PCC) and the population of this study was the International City/County Management Association's (ICMA) annual meeting attendees. Overall, 217 out of 400 attendees were used for analysis, providing a response rate of 54 percent.

Here are your two questions. Circle one for each question: T = true, F = false, ? = topic and answer does not appear in Chapter 3. You receive one point for each correct answer.

1. T F? It would be a challenge for the marketing managers to interpret service attributes rated higher than desired expectation, because two ways are available to read such findings: possible overkill versus delighted performance.
2. T F? Both (IPA and ZOT) techniques mainly utilize the means (actual or scale) of the service quality attributes; however, researchers and practitioners need to assess the attributes' standard deviations before employing either technique to assess their performance and customer expectations.
3. T F? Both IPA and ZOT findings need to be supplemented by using the "think aloud" method to learn individual respondent's rationales for the assessment assignments.

Luxury Tourists: Celebrities' Perspectives

In Chapter 4, Antónia Correia, Metin Kozak, and Helena Reis seek, first to assess how individuals with a high socioeconomic status (the contemporary lavish society — Portuguese Celebrities) perceived tourism luxuries; second, to analyze how they experience luxuries in tourism, since for these individuals, luxury is a feature of the manner of traveling rather than necessarily of the destination they are traveling to; third, to enlighten us on whether their inner concept of luxury tourism differs from their everyday meanings of luxury; and fourth, to understand to what extent luxury relates to outrageous or excessive spending and these individuals' willingness to assume this in an explicit way. The authors are able to identify three segments participating in luxury travel: Musicians, Reporters, and Socialites.

Your need to answer now multiple choice questions before reading the chapter. You receive one point for each correct answer. Circle one letter provided for each question.

1. A B C The Musicians on average tended to (a) value snobbism less than conformity, (b) emphasize most the hedonic value of their holidays, (c) be the snobbiest group, their distinctive attitude focusing on gaining social status and pleasure.
2. A B C The Reporters on average tended to (a) value snobbism less than conformity, (b) emphasize most the hedonic value of their holidays, (c) be the snobbiest group, their distinctive attitude focusing on gaining social status and pleasure.
3. A B C Socialites on average tended to tended to (a) value snobbism less than conformity, (b) emphasize most the hedonic value of their holidays, (c) be the snobbiest group, their distinctive attitude focusing on gaining social status and pleasure.

Nontrivial Behavioral Implications of Trivial Design Choices in Travel Websites

In Chapter 5, Eyal Ert presents three empirical examples demonstrating surprising effects of trivial design choices: the consequence of presenting items in a list which creates "mere position effects," the consequence of presenting attributes in categories that might create "partitioning effects," and the consequence of using certain backgrounds which might create "priming effects." Each of these examples demonstrates how even trivial (supposedly neutral) design choices directly affect the customer's decision-making process and may alter his or her choices.

Here are two questions to answer before reading Chapter 5. Each correct answer is worth one point.

1. Circle the worst position location in a list of ten hotels given to a tourist to select a place to stay:
  1 2 3 4 5 6 7 8 9 10.
2. Circle one choice: Higher Lower The same: Participants in a study read the recipe for a Japanese roll; it was found that when the recipe was written in a "hard to read" font (Mistral, 12), participants rated the skills of the restaurant's chef as higher/lower/the same than when the dish was described in an "easy to read" font (Ariel, 12) (5.2 and 4.1, respectively, on a 7-point rating scale).

The Role of Social Psychology in the Tourism Experience Model (TEM)

In Chapter 6 Juergen Gnoth explains that the TEM ("Tourism Experience Model") seeks an understanding of how the individual actually experiences any interactions, whether within social, natural, or introspective environments. Although the description and analysis of such experiencing can gain further depth by utilizing concepts and constructs of social and cultural psychology, the discussion highlights that the TEM also includes the existential self which, historically, is said to emerge as part of ongoing individualization. By highlighting how an individual may be experiencing his environment as a function of consciousness and activity, the TEM can show if and how the experience consolidates, recreates, or rediscovers previously made experiences, or whether the individual is involved in learning and exploration.

One question to answer here. This essay question is worth five points. The correct answer is worth five points. Here is the question: Compare and contract TEM and the tourist gaze. Is the TEM the antithesis of the tourist gaze or not? If yes, how can the conundrum be resolved? If not, why not?

Assessing National Destination-Branding Transformations:
Theory and Application to Costa Rica's Nature-Based and Medical
Tourism Product-Services

In Chapter 7, Rodrigo Murillo assesses the medical industry and then medical tourism industries on a global basis and the US market is examined in detail because of its potential to develop a new complementary niche for Costa Rica's tourism industry. The chapter intends to asses Costa Rica's potential to become a country brand in medical tourism, leveraged on its natural tourism destination-branding status quo. Chapter 7 is the lengthiest chapter in the volume and takes an outside-the-box assessment of tourists' perceptions and assessments.

Here are two questions to answer before reading Chapter 7. Circle one answer for each question. T = true; F = false; ? = uncertain. Each correct answer is worth one point. No penalty for guessing if you have no idea.

1. T   F? Medical tourism globally has completed the take-off stage of development.
2. T   F? Medical tourism revenues in Costa Rica have doubled during 2010−2013.

Destination Brand Performance Measurement over Time

In Chapter 8, Steven Pike provides key findings from a study of brand performance of a competitive set of destinations, in their most important market, between 2003 and 2012. Brand performance was measured from the
perspective of consumer perceptions, based on the concept of consumer-
based brand equity (CBBE). The results indicate almost no change in
perceptions of the five destinations over the 10-year period. Due to the
commonality of challenges faced by DMOs worldwide, the CBBE hierarchy provides destination marketers with a practical tool for evaluating
brand performance over time; in terms of measures of effectiveness of past
marketing communications, as well as indicators of future performance.

Here are two true/false/? questions to answer before reading Chapter 8.
Each correct answer is worth two points.

1. T F? In the United States, of 47 state slogans used by US STOs in 1982
   (see Pritchard, 1982) only 11 were in use in 1993 (see Richardson &
   Cohen, 1993).
2. T F? Of those slogans being used in 1993, only 3 were still being used in
   2003.

Perceptions of Hotel Disintermediation: The French Generation Y Case

In Chapter 9, Girish Prayag and Giacomo Del Chiappa examine
Generation Y travelers' perceptions of hotel disintermediation in France.
The results, based on a sample of 378 French travelers, show four underlying dimensions of perceptions. Findings also reveal that only gender and
age significantly influence perceptions. The chapter closes with implications
for increasing trust and attractiveness of the online accommodation offer
to French Generation Y.

Here are two true/false/? questions to answer before reading Chapter 9.
Each correct answer is worth two points. Circle one of three possible
answers for each question.

1. T F? Education has a greater impact than age as a significant influence
   on tourists' perceptions and assessments of hotels during their online
   searches.
2. T F? Young travelers in general are mostly favorable toward the role of
   travel agencies in providing services that they value for accommodation
   booking.

Constructing and Shaping Tourist Experiences via Travel Blog Engagement

In Chapter 10, Nik Alia Wan Ab Rahman, Sangkyun Kim, and Steve Brown propose a theoretical framework that provides a holistic understanding of the role of tourists' engagement with travel blogs in constructing and shaping tourism experiences at the three different stages of tourist experiences. They add to the existing tourist experiences literature by applying a longitudinal approach to understand tourism experiences that are constantly and simultaneously constructed, shaped, and packaged at all three different stages of tourist experiences in the context of travel blogs.

Please answer the following two questions before reading Chapter 10. Doing so correctly is worth two points for each question.

1. T F? Socio-demographics and motivation are two important factors that influence people's engagement with social media.
2. T F? The big shortcoming of prior studies examining blog reports is that they use only one evaluator per blog analysis.

Facilitators and Constraints in the Participation of Women in Golf

In Chapter 11, Helena Reis and Antónia Correia analyze the facilitators and constraints women golfers face. The research presents 33 intrapersonal, interpersonal, and structural factors, being supported by a theoretical sampling and data triangulation. Their findings indicate that all participants perceive factors that moderate their participation and highlight dissimilar perceptions by professional and amateur players. Contributions address a manifest heterogeneity: social values prevail even when women are encouraged to join leisure activities. Study limitations derive from the geographical scope restricted to Portugal, yet raising awareness to gender in golf.

Here are two true/false/? questions to answer for Chapter 11. Please answer before reading the chapter. Each correct answer is worth two points.

1. T F? When comparing women golf profiles within the amateur group, friends are a great motivator for single women in comparison to married women with children, who do not have much time to socialize.
2. T F? Family obligations are more verbalized by women over 50, maybe due to the burdens imposed on women with families.

Hospitality Meanings and Consequences among Hotels Employees and Guests

In Chapter 12, Hamida Skandrani and Mariem Kamoun aim to identify the representations of hospitality among guests and hotels employees and to uncover hospitality consequences on guests' intention and behavior. Their qualitative approach increases understanding of people and the social and cultural contexts within which they live. To achieve the study objectives, we take into account not only the point of view of hotels employees but also the Tunisian and Foreigner guests. This multi-actors approach offers a better understanding of the hospitality representations among key actors in the Tunisian context, acknowledged to be hospitable. Hotels employees were selected from diverse types of hotels in Tunisia, 9 hotels belong to international hotel chains and 7 hotels belong to national hotel chains, 7 out of 23 hotels are private.

Here are two questions to answer before reading Chapter 12. Each correct answer is worth two points. Please answer before reading the chapter.

1. T F? The results show that hotel room cleanliness is the major dimension of hospitableness.
2. T   F? Appreciation tokens such as welcoming drinks or gifts upon checking-in at the reception are considered as means to create surprise and excitement in the hotel hospitality by the employees but they are turn-offs among guests in 5-star hotels.

Reflections on Destination Positioning Analyses and Identifying Competitors

In Chapter 13, Andreas H. Zins proposes an innovative procedure on how to collect profile data on individually relevant destination alternatives. Its main objective is the application of the simultaneous segmentation and positioning analysis of a destination including its competitors. This technique is called perception-based market segmentation.

Here are the final two questions to answer in the pre-reading quiz. Each correct answer is worth two points. Please answer before reading the chapter.

1. T F? In the study that Chapter 13 reports, the majority of travelers (around 80%) reported that they had only one destination in mind

(Thailand) when planning the trip (no significant differences between actual and prospective travelers).

2. T F? Prospective travelers report having about three (±2) destinations in mind but the majority of actual travelers report having only one destination in mind.

GENERAL CONCLUSION

We appreciate your active involvement in reading this volume, *Tourists' Perceptions and Assessments*, by answering the questions at the end of Chapters 2 through 13. Send your answers to the coeditors and we will reply with a copy of the correct answers. If you answers include 20 + correct responses you will receive the HETPA Award. The editors hope that you find the format and contents of Volume 8 in the ACTHR series to be engaging and insightful. If yes, please consider submitting your own paper on creating and testing theory on culture, tourism, and hospitality research. If not, consider taking the same action − submit your own research for publication consideration in the next volume.

We close with our deep expression of gratitude for the members of the expanded ACTHR Editorial Advisory Board. With their heavy commitment in time and efforts in writing the anonymous reviews on the submissions, Volume 8 could not have been completed. While often appearing at first blush to be a thankless task, the work of the members of the EAB is essential for the success of the ACTHR book series. Thank you!

The editors also appreciate the editorial team at Emerald for their encouragement and continuing contact/asking about the completion status of Volume 8. Both the encouragement and peskiness are much appreciated. Thank you!

REFERENCES

Baker, B., & Peggy Bendel, P. (2005). *Come and say G'Day! Travel marketing decisions. The association of travel marketing executives*. Retrieved from http://www.atme.org/pubs/archives/77_1898_11926.cfm. Accessed on February 15, 2014.

Bargh, J. A. (1982). Attention and automaticity in the processing of self-relevant information. *Journal of Personality and Social Psychology*, 49, 1040–1053.

Bargh, J. A., & Chartrand, T. L. (1999). The unbearable automaticity of being. *American Psychologist*, 54, 462–479.

Bargh, J. A., Chen, M., & Burrows, L. (1996). Automaticity of social behavior: Direct effects of trait construct and stereotype activation on action. *Journal of Personality and Social Psychology*, *71*, 230–244.

Brit ban on "bloody" ad "incredibly ludicrous". (2009). *The Sydney Morning Herald*. March 28, 2007.

Hofstede, G. (2001). *Culture's consequences* (Rev. ed.) Beverly Hills, CA: Sage.

Hsu, S., Woodside, A. G., & Marshall, R. (2013). Critical tests of multiple theories of cultures' consequences comparing the usefulness of models by Hofstede, Inglehart and Baker, Schwartz, Steenkamp, as well as GDP and distance for explaining overseas tourism behavior. *Journal of Travel Research*, *52*, 679–704.

Jenks, C. (2004). *Culture*. Oxon, UK: Routledge.

Jung, C. G. (1916/1959). The archetypes and the collective unconscious. In H. Read, M. Fordham, & G. Adler (Eds.), *Collective works* (Vol. 9, Pt. 1). Princeton, NJ: Princeton University Press.

Jung, C. G. (2009). *The red book*. New York, NY: Norton.

MacKay, K. J., & Fesenmaier, D. R. (2000). An exploration of cross-cultural destination image assessment. *Journal of Travel Research*, *38*, 417–423.

Muziani, H. (2006). Backpacking Southeast Asia: Strategies of "looking local". *Annals of Tourism Research*, *33*, 144–161.

Pitts, R. J., & Woodside, A. G. (1986). Personal values influence on destination choice. *Journal of Travel Research*, *25*, 20–25.

Ragin, C. (2008). *Redesigning social inquiry: Fuzzy sets and beyond*. Chicago, IL: Chicago University Press.

Richardson, J., & Cohen, J. (1993). State slogans: The case of the missing USP. *Journal of Travel & Tourism Marketing*, *2*(2–3), 91–109.

Urry, J. (1992). The tourist gaze and the "environment". *Theory Culture & Society*, *9*, 1–26.

Urry, J., & Larsen, J. (2011). *The tourist gaze 3.0*. Thousand Oaks, CA: Sage.

Wertime, K. (2002). *Building brands and believers: How to connect with consumers using archetypes*. Singapore: Wiley.

Wikipedia. (2014). Retrieved from http://en.wikipedia.org/wiki/Where_the_bloody_hell_are_ you. Accessed on April 29, 2014.

Williams, L. E., & Bargh, J. A. (2008). Experiencing physical warmth promotes interpersonal warmth. *Science*, *322*, 606–607.

Woodside, A. G. (2008). Using the forced metaphor-elicitation technique (FMET) to meet animal companions within self. *Journal of Business Research*, *61*, 480–487.

Woodside, A. G. (2010). *Case study research: Theory, methods and practice*. Bingley, UK: Emerald.

Woodside, A. G. (2013). Moving beyond multiple regression analysis to algorithms: Calling for a paradigm shift from symmetrical to asymmetrical data analysis and Crafting theory. *Journal of Business Research*, *66*, 463–472.

Woodside, A. G., & Glenesk, G. (1984). Thought processing of advertisements in low versus high noise conditions. *Journal of Advertising*, *13*, 4–33.

Woodside, A. G., Hsu, S.-Y., & Marshall, R. (2011). General theory of cultures' consequences on international tourism behavior. *Journal of Business Research*, *64*, 785–799.

Zaltman, G. (2003). *How customers think: Essential insights into the mind of the markets*. Boston, MA: Harvard Business School Press.

Zaltman, G., & Zaltman, L. (2008). *Marketing metaphoria: What deep metaphors reveal about the minds of consumers*. Cambridge, MA: Harvard Business Review Press.

CHAPTER 2

NATIONALITY DIFFERENCES IN USER-GENERATED REVIEWS IN THE HOSPITALITY INDUSTRY

Maria D. Alvarez and Burçin Hatipoğlu

ABSTRACT

The chapter investigates the evaluation and rating practice of individual travelers, through the examination of user-generated comments on the Internet. The study focuses on determining the most mentioned attributes of the accommodation experience, with consideration given to nationality differences. The individual evaluations of 40 Istanbul hotels are examined through an analysis of guest comments and hotel ratings posted in the Booking.com web site. The results obtained through content analysis provide knowledge to the accommodation industry in Istanbul regarding the areas in need of improvement, with consideration to variations among guests from different nationalities.

Keywords: User-generated content; online travel reviews; hotel attributes; accommodation

Tourists' Perceptions and Assessments
Advances in Culture, Tourism and Hospitality Research, Volume 8, 23–29
ISSN: 1871-3173/doi:10.1108/S1871-317320140000008000

INTRODUCTION

Electronic word-of-mouth is becoming increasingly more important for the hospitality industry, since those hotels that achieve better ratings in web-based reviews tend to obtain higher revenues (Bender-Stringam, Gerdes, & Vanleeuwen, 2010). Researchers have also discovered that blogs and reviews can be used to understand the tourists' consumption experiences (Chan & Denizci-Guillet, 2011). However, there is still limited knowledge regarding how individuals differ in their online evaluations, especially in terms of nationality and cultural background. Therefore, the purpose of the study is to explore nationality differences in the post-consumption review behavior of hotel customers through an analysis of guest comments and hotel ratings posted in the Booking.com web site.

THEORETICAL CONSIDERATIONS

Accommodation establishments are ever more concerned with the quality of their services in an increasingly competitive environment. According to previous research, customers perceive and evaluate services as a collection of attributes, which may vary in their contributions to overall service quality and product choice (Choi & Chu, 2001). Cultural and nationality differences have been found relevant in this topic (Mattila, 1999). Within the context of travel services, a study (Crotts & Erdmann, 2000) determined that individuals from masculine cultures are more assertive and likely to be critical in their evaluations. Examining variations in perceptions and satisfaction of individuals from diverse nationalities is also found useful for segmentation purposes and to determine the most adequate strategies to address each segment (Kozak, 2002).

The evaluation of consumption experiences has changed radically with the emergence of the Internet and electronic word-of-mouth. However, online reviews are not only an important source of information for travelers, but they also constitute very valuable input for organizations (Papathanassis & Knolle, 2011). Several studies have focused on analyzing the determinants of customer satisfaction in the hospitality industry through a review of online hotel customer reviews (Magnini, Crotts, & Zehrer, 2011). However, there is a lack of research investigating whether these key attributes may be different for individuals from diverse nationalities and cultural backgrounds.

METHOD

The research explores difference patterns in review behavior among nationalities. The study is based on the case of the Istanbul accommodation industry, so that 40 hotels from different categories were selected and information concerning the guest-generated reviews in the Booking.com web site for these establishments was retrieved. All the reviews and average hotel ratings posted in the site for the selected hotels between April and June 2012 were collected. In total, comments and average hotel scores from 1,154 guests were obtained. Among the reviews, 777 remarks were positive, while 825 were negative. Each customer average hotel evaluation score on a 10-point scale was also collected. In this study, word frequency and content analysis were used in order to analyze the positive and negative comments collected, using NVivo 9. The analysis resulted in a list of items and categories, including the number of references to specific accommodation issues (see Table 1).

FINDINGS

The research provides information on the most frequently mentioned accommodation attributes; both positive and negative (refer to Table 1). The most often cited items are hotel location, friendliness of employees, the breakfast at the hotel, cleanliness and hygiene, level of noise, matching of customer expectations, service quality, size of the room, hotel view, and price. The research findings also provide information about the most positive and negative aspects of the hotel industry in Istanbul. Customers valued most the location, the friendliness of employees, and the view from the hotel in their accommodation experience in Istanbul. The most frequent negative references relate to the rooms being too loud, the breakfast provided, and the amenities and toiletries in the room. These results provide knowledge to the accommodation industry in Istanbul regarding the areas in need of improvement.

In order to determine whether or not discrepancies among reviews from customers of different nationalities exist, the comments for individuals from the 10 first countries in terms of population size in the sample were analyzed. Table 2 provides a summary of the number of comments, both positive and negative for guests coming from these countries. Significant differences between nationalities are found in the number of positive

Table 1. Summary Categorization and Frequencies of Customer Coded References.

Categories and Items	Positive Frequency	Negative Frequency	Total Frequency
Room attributes	476	323	799
Cleanliness and hygiene	202	20	222
Level of noise	65	86	151
Size of the room	82	50	132
Room decoration	71	12	83
Amenities and toiletries	18	64	82
Bathroom	38	33	71
Air conditioning/heating	0	38	38
Odor	0	20	20
Hotel attributes	685	82	767
Location	481	31	512
View	108	21	129
Design (lobby, building)	52	6	58
Renovation	17	23	40
Atmosphere	18	0	18
Security level	9	1	10
Hotel services	364	266	630
Breakfast	182	69	251
Other facilities (pool, fitness, etc.)	41	39	80
Restaurant	58	18	76
Wi-Fi	26	47	73
Reception/front office	27	34	61
Other general services	13	44	57
Transfer service	17	15	32
Employee behavior and services	405	124	529
Friendliness/helpfulness/politeness	264	32	296
Service quality	78	55	133
Competence/professionalism	50	10	60
Language skills	13	27	40
Customer expectations (matching/not matching)	103	35	138
Price	80	40	120
Customer intentions	87	13	100
Intention to recommend	52	6	58
Intention to return	35	7	42
Total number of references	2,200	883	3,083

Table 2. Ratio of Positive/Negative/Total Coded References to Population Size by Nationality.

Country[a]	Number of Respondents	Number of Positive References	Ratio of Positive References to Total Number of Respondents	Number of Negative References	Ratio of Negative References to Total Number of Respondents	Number of Total References	Ratio of Total References to Total Number of Respondents	Ratio of Positive to Negative References	Average Hotel Evaluation Scores
1. France	56	146	2.61	63	1.13	209	3.73	2.32	7.86
2. Netherlands	44	109	2.48	41	0.93	150	3.41	2.66	8.13
3. Germany	80	195	2.44	74	0.93	269	3.36	2.64	7.87
4. United Kingdom	47	100	2.13	42	0.89	142	3.02	2.38	8.29
5. Greece	44	93	2.11	37	0.84	130	2.95	2.51	8.01
6. Italy	55	128	2.33	29	0.53	157	2.85	4.41	7.93
7. United Arab Emirates	55	82	1.49	55	1.00	137	2.49	1.49	7.78
8. Saudi Arabia	98	154	1.57	78	0.80	232	2.37	1.97	7.84
9. Turkey	144	247	1.72	93	0.65	340	2.36	2.66	7.85
10. Russia	64	106	1.66	41	0.64	147	2.30	2.59	8.40

[a]Only the first 10 countries in the sample in terms of number of respondents are analyzed. The countries are sorted in terms of percentage of total references to population (highest to lowest).

($F = 4.778$, $p = 0.000$) and negative references ($F = 2.177$, $p = 0.022$) provided. According to the findings, the four Western nations (France, Netherlands, Germany, and United Kingdom) appear to be more vocal than the Eastern countries in the sample (Russia, Turkey, Saudi Arabia, and United Arab Emirates).

Additionally, the research determines that for customers coming from Northern countries (namely Russia, Germany, United Kingdom, and the Netherlands) one of the most negative aspects of their accommodation experience is the level of noise in the room. In contrast, for guests coming from Saudi Arabia, United Arab Emirates, Turkey, or Greece this issue is less critical. Location of the hotel, cleanliness of the room, and friendliness of the employees is mentioned by customers from the various nationalities analyzed. Among the negative comments, some variation among nationalities exists in terms of the importance given to the size of the room (most critical for guests from Saudi Arabia, Italy, and Greece) and the existence of other services at the hotel (most valued by Turkish and Saudi Arabian customers). These results can provide guidance to Istanbul hotels as to which attributes they should focus on to provide a better experience to guests from different nationalities.

CONCLUSION AND IMPLICATIONS

The research provides both practical and theoretical implications. From an academic perspective, the study explores the topic of guest-generated reviews and ratings of accommodation establishments in Istanbul, indicating national differences in the post-consumption evaluation behavior. In particular, the research points to variations in the way that individuals express themselves when reviewing a hotel, and in the attributes that are most mentioned by customers coming from diverse national backgrounds.

ACKNOWLEDGMENT

The authors acknowledge the support to this research provided by the Boğaziçi University Scientific Research Projects Fund (Project code: BAP − 6510).

REFERENCES

Bender-Stringam, B., Gerdes, J., & Vanleeuwen, D. M. (2010). Assessing the importance and relationships of ratings on user-generated traveler reviews. *Journal of Quality Assurance in Hospitality & Tourism, 11*(2), 73−92.

Chan, N. L., & Denizci-Guillet, B. (2011). Investigation of social media marketing: how does the hotel industry in Hong Kong perform in marketing on social media websites? *Journal of Travel & Tourism Marketing, 28*(4), 345−368.

Choi, T. R., & Chu, R. (2001). Determinants of hotel guests' satisfaction and repeat patronage in the Hong Kong hotel industry. *International Journal of Hospitality Management, 20*(3), 277−297.

Crotts, J. C., & Erdmann, R. (2000). Does national culture influence consumers' evaluation of travel services? A test of Hofstede's model of cross-cultural differences. *Managing Service Quality, 10*(6), 410−419.

Kozak, M. (2002). Comparative analysis of tourist motivations by nationality and destinations. *Tourism Management, 23*, 221−232.

Magnini, V. P., Crotts, J. C., & Zehrer, A. (2011). Understanding customer delight: An application of travel blog analysis. *Journal of Travel Research, 50*(5), 535−545.

Mattila, A. S. (1999). The role of culture in the service evaluation process. *Journal of Service Research, 1*(3), 250−261.

Papathanassis, A., & Knolle, F. (2011). Exploring the adoption and processing of online holiday reviews: A grounded theory approach. *Tourism Management, 32*, 215−224.

CHAPTER 3

EVALUATION OF THE SERVICE PERFORMANCE: APPLICATIONS OF THE ZONE OF TOLERANCE WITH IMPORTANCE-PERFORMANCE ANALYSIS

Hwansuk Chris Choi, Woojin Lee, HeeKyung Sung and Chien-Fen Chiu

ABSTRACT

This study compares the applicability of the zone of tolerance and importance-performance analysis (IPA) techniques in the evaluation of convention delegates' perceptions of products and services. Overall, 217 cases out of 400 were used for analysis, a response rate of 54 percent. The study results indicate that although an IPA technique is still useful in assessing the service performance of a convention facility, IPA should be employed with caution, concrete criteria, and clear goals. The study

Tourists' Perceptions and Assessments
Advances in Culture, Tourism and Hospitality Research, Volume 8, 31–41
Copyright © 2014 by Emerald Group Publishing Limited
ISSN: 1871-3173/doi:10.1108/S1871-317320140000008012

results also show that the zone of tolerance is practically applicable into business practice to assess service performance item by item.

Keywords: Zone of tolerance; importance-performance analysis; three-factor theory; service quality; convention center

INTRODUCTION

Prior convention research focuses on the economic impact of the convention industry and the decision-making process concerning the convention site (Crouch & Ritchie, 1998). Given the growing competiveness of the convention industry, a thorough understanding of service performance has become more important than ever. Along with this trend, recent convention studies examine attendees' needs, service performance (quality) factors, service priorities, and motivations (Severt, Wang, Chen, & Beriter, 2007). It is critical for organizations to build their strategies with attention to key factors in service performance.

To develop and implement a strategic approach, organizations need to understand how their customers perceive the key elements of service performance. Several models and methods have been used in marketing research. One proven method is importance-performance analysis (IPA). The IPA provides strategically useful information to take corrective action, and build and maintain competitive advantages. Another technique used to assess service performance is zone of tolerance (ZOT), which is a range of customers' expectations of service (Zeithaml, Berry, & Parasuraman, 1993). This chapter examines convention delegates' perceptions of product and service performance of a convention facility by applying IPA and ZOT.

THEORETICAL CONSIDERATIONS

Importance-Performance Analysis

As the convention industry becomes increasingly competitive, delivering quality service is essential (e.g., Randall & Senior, 1994). Therefore, the level of service quality affects an organization's competitiveness and performance and has been an important topic for research. One increasingly popular method used to assess the quality of service is the IPA, which examines customers' acceptance of product and service attributes (Martilla & James, 1977).

Formulated by Martilla and James (1977), IPA views satisfaction in terms of the importance of service attributes to customers, as well as the performance of a service provider. These combined satisfaction ratings are plotted on a two-dimensional action grid, where the level of importance on the vertical axes and the level of performance on the horizontal axes of service attributes are compared (Joppe, Martin, & Waalen, 2001).

The Zone of Tolerance

The ZOT is a range of customers' expectations of service (Zeithaml et al., 1993). The ZOT provides information not only about customers' perceptions of service quality but also about the discrepancy between the desired services and those that are actually provided. Parasuraman, Berry, and Zeithaml (1991) applied SERVQUAL when assessing service performance by utilizing ZOT. Traditionally, researchers focused on the desired expectation as the only comparison standard to measure the gap between expectation and service quality (Walker & Baker, 2000).

To understand customers' service expectations, Parasuraman et al. (1991) propose two levels of service expectation: desired and adequate service. Desired expectation is the level of service that customers wish to receive; adequate service is the minimum level of service that customers are willing to accept (Parasuraman et al., 1991). Adequate service is not as good as desired service, and the separation between the two is the "zone of tolerance" (Parasuraman, 2004). Hence, if customers' perceived level of service falls within the zone, they are still satisfied with service delivered (i.e., competitive advantage). If the service is better than the level of desire service, customers consider the service to be outstanding (i.e., customer franchise). However, if the service is less than adequate, customers are dissatisfied (i.e., competitive disadvantage) (Parasuraman, 2004; Parasuraman et al., 1991).

Three-Factor Theory

Many studies report that the five dimensions of service quality are unstable (e.g., Campos & Nobrega, 2009). In such, some researchers have suggested that service performance can be better measured with two or three dimensions. Matzler and Sauerwein (2002) suggest a comprehensive, three-factor structure of customer satisfaction based on previous research on customer satisfaction: basic, performance, and excitement. Basic factors are minimum requirements that cause dissatisfaction if not fulfilled, but do not lead to customer satisfaction if fulfilled or exceeded (p. 318). It is not a sufficient condition for satisfaction; rather, it is a threshold in order to enter the market (Füller & Matzler, 2008).

At the same time, performance factors link directly to customers' needs and desires; consequently, performance factors lead to satisfaction if fulfilled or exceeded, and lead to dissatisfaction if not. Excitement factors increase customer satisfaction if services are delivered, but do not cause dissatisfaction if they are missing (Füller & Matzler, 2008; Matzler & Sauerwein, 2002). Since these services are provided to customers beyond their needs and expectations, there is nothing to decrease their satisfaction. With these points in mind, this study adopts Füller and Matzler's three-factor structure of service quality.

METHOD

Service quality items for a convention facility were extracted from the review of literature. Based on the consultation and pretest, 25 out of 38 services were selected for a survey questionnaire to test attendees' perceived level of importance and their perception of service performance. The study data were collected at the Phoenix Convention Center (PCC) and the population of this study was the International City/County Management Association's (ICMA) annual meeting attendees. Overall, 217 out of 400 attendees were used for analysis, providing a response rate of 54 percent.

FINDINGS

IPA Results

Fig. 1(a–e), represents the "Importance/Performance Matrix." The average scores, neutral values, and grand means of each factor – basic, performance, and excitement – of the raw and actual performance were used as references in the IPA matrix. Based on the conservative IPA results appear in Fig. 1(a), 11 basic factor attributes fell into Quadrant II, except parking service (importance = 3.97 and performance = 4.70). Among seven performance service attributes, local food facilities and accommodation also fell into Quadrant II ("keep up the good work"). Four performance service attributes (in-house food service, business service, accommodation, and food quality) were considered as low-priority areas of service provision. General food outlet is the only attribute that needs to be improved, including all the attributes in the other two factors. The entire set of excited factor attributes fall into either the low priority ("nightlife, cultural atmosphere, special food, and tourist information") and possible overkill ("green efforts and light trail") quadrant.

Fig. 1(b) demonstrates the neutral point data (4 on a 7-point, Likert-type scale) plotting of the importance and performance scores with horizontal and vertical gridlines, and the results are quite different from the

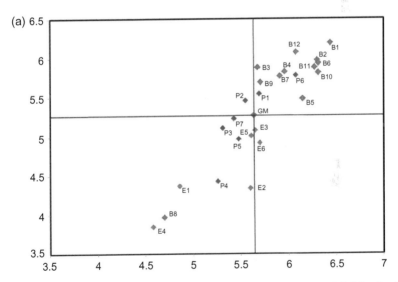

Fig. 1. Results of Data Analysis: IPA & ZoT. (a) Conservative IPA Matrix; (b) Liberal IPA Matrix; (c) IPA Matrix by Basic Factor; (d) IPA Matrix by Performance Factor; (e) IPA Matrix by Excitement Factor; (f) ZOT Analysis Result. *Note: Basic factor* – B1: cleanliness; B2: maintenance; B3: comfort seat; B4: ventilation; B5: public space; B6: restroom access; B7: Wi-Fi availability; B8: parking service; B9: signage; B10: friendly staff; B11: helpful staff; B12: safety. *Performance factor* – P1: local food facilities; P2: general food outlet; P3: in-house food; P4: business service; P5: road signage; P6: accommodation; P7: food quality. *Excitement factor* – E1: nightlife; E2: cultural atmosphere; E3: green effort; E4: special food; E5: tourist information; E6: light trail.

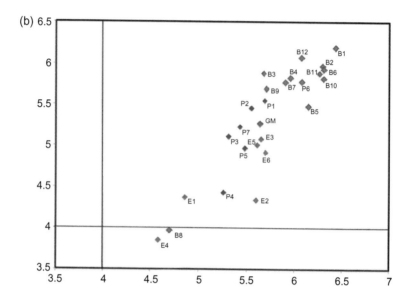

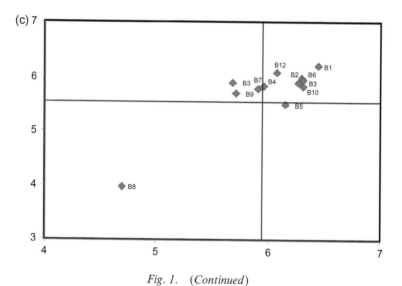

Fig. 1. (*Continued*)

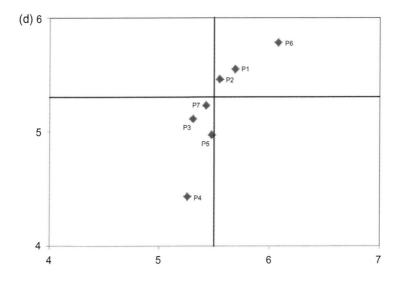

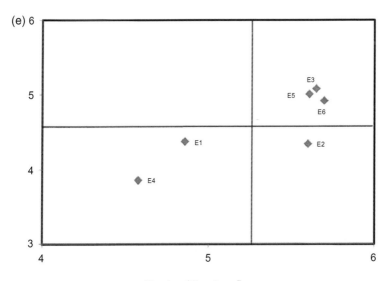

Fig. 1. (Continued)

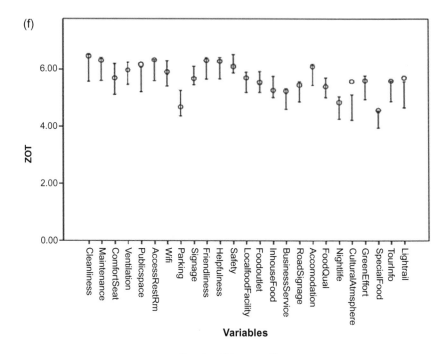

Fig. 1. (Continued)

conservative (traditional) IPA results above. All but two service quality attributes are located in Quadrant II ("high satisfaction, high importance"); the exceptions are parking service in the basic factor and special food in the excitement factor, falling into Quadrant IV ("possible overkill").

Fig. 1(c–e) are importance-performance matrixes showing the overall ratings of convention delegates' perceptions of PCC, using each factor's grand means. The basic factor IPA grid shows some critical differences from the results of conservative IPA. Service attributes, including comfortable seating, Wi-Fi availability, and signage fell under the heading of "concentrate efforts" here, while public space has achieved a high level of performance, but it has been over-invested ("possible overkill"). Furthermore, the performance factor IPA results also provide the different results from the conservative IPA results.

Three service quality attributes (local food facilities, general food outlet, and accommodation) fell into the "keep up the good work" quadrant. From the results of the conservative (traditional) IPA, no service attributes of the excitement factors were displayed in Quadrant II ("high importance, high performance") when applying the grand means as a cross-hair point. However, by utilizing the grand means of the excitement factor attributes (liberal IPA), green efforts, tourist information, and light trail fell into the keep up the good work quadrant, which provides the conflict results from the conservative IPA results.

ZOT Analysis Results

Fig. 1(f) presents the ZOT for the 25 service attributes in the box plot while the top and the bottom of the boxes are the means of respondents' desired and minimum level of expectations; additionally, the middle band represents the means of respondents' perceived service performance. Most of the respondents' perceived service performance was located within the Zones of Tolerance, which were close to the desired expectations at the top of the boxes, meaning that the respondents were highly satisfied. Exceptions were public space in the basic factor, as well as light trail and cultural atmosphere, which indicate that the PCC's performance was higher than the respondents' desired expectations, representing possible overkill.

In addition, four service attributes were relatively close to the minimum level of the delegates' perceived performance when compared with the other services: parking service, signage, safety, and in-house food. In other words, some of the respondents were unsatisfied with these four service attributes provided by PCC. In such, PCC's performance failed to meet the minimum expectation of a certain segment of the respondents. This ZOT analysis result is equivalent to the concentrated efforts in the IPA matrix.

CONCLUSION AND IMPLICATIONS

IPA should be employed with caution, concrete criteria, and clear goals — this is the key lesson learned from this study's results. The study's findings show that the improper use of the IPA application (i.e., the use of different cross-hair points) may lead to possible misinterpretation of the IPA analysis results. In such, defining a cross-hair point indicating high importance and high performance is a management decision based on the management team's experience and strategic goals.

The conservative IPA results show that most excitement factors fall into the low-priority quadrant, while the excitement factor IPA results in three attributes within the high-importance and high-performance category. The results of performance factor attributes for the two different approaches show similar results. In addition, most attributes fall in the "keep up the good work" quadrant in the liberal IPA results when employing neutral values as cross-hair points. Thus, without setting clear criteria and goals, these conflicting results can easily influence misleading interpretation of the study results. The IPA user must interpret the results with caution and pre-defined criteria. Furthermore, for practical use, a factor-based approach may work better than a conservative (traditional) approach, especially when applying a three-factor theory, because, unlike the equally important nature of a 5-dimension service quality, the basic structure of a three-factor theory is hierarchical in nature.

Utilizing the multiple-expectation standards, the ZOT-enabled technique allows researchers and practitioners to deepen our understanding of customers' service expectations and to explore customers' tolerance levels toward each single service. Despite the fact that basic services have a narrower tolerance zone, respondents actually have the narrowest tolerance zone toward the performance services (zone width = .71) and have quite similar tolerance zones toward basic (zone width = .78) and excitement services (zone width = .80). This result indicates that the study respondents are relatively insensitive to both basic service and excitement factors. Performance factor attributes may be critical factors in building competitive advantages for PCC. Overall, the ZOT analysis results indicate that PCC provide high-quality service to their customers. However, it would be a challenge for the marketing managers to interpret service attributes rated higher than desired expectation, because two ways are available to read such findings: possible overkill versus delighted performance. Thus marketing managers should interpret the results with caution and with consideration of the organization's resource allocation and strategic goals.

Both techniques mainly utilize the means (actual or scale) of the service quality attributes; however, researchers and practitioners need to assess the attributes' standard deviations before employing either technique to assess their performance and customer expectations. Standard deviation is a useful tool to assess the dispersion of the study data. In other words, if the study data intervals (i.e., $-s < x < +s$) of certain service quality attributes are relatively large, that indicates a significant variation in responses. In practical terms, the service quality attributes with large standard deviation imply a possible discrepancy between certain groups toward expectation and performance; for example, satisfied versus unsatisfied, first time versus repeat visitors, delegates versus exhibitors or type of event attended that is held in a convention center (i.e., consumer and trade show, convention and conference). For instance, excitement factor attributes have relatively large standard deviations of both importance (ranging from 1.29 to 2.00) and performance (ranging from 1.13 to 1.75). Then, a segment-based analysis should be applied for both techniques. In this sense, both techniques can be used as a tool for identifying potential areas to be improved and to be used as a way to build competitive advantages at the initial stage of the strategic goal assessment.

REFERENCES

Campos, D. F., & Nobrega, K. C. (2009). Importance and zone of tolerance of customer expectations of fast food services. *The Flagship Research Journal of International Conference of the Production and Operations Management Society, 2*(2), 56–71.

Crouch, G. I., & Ritchie, J. R. B. (1998). Convention site selection research: A review, conceptual model, and propositional framework. *Journal of Convention and Exhibition Management, 1*(1), 49–69.

Füller, J., & Matzler, K. (2008). Customer delight and market segmentation: An application of the three-factor theory of customer satisfaction on life style groups. *Tourism Management, 29*(1), 116.

Joppe, M., Martin, D. W., & Waalen, J. (2001). Toronto's image as a destination: A comparative importance-satisfaction analysis by origin of visitor. *Journal of Travel Research, 39*(1), 252–260.

Martilla, J., & James, J. (1977). Importance-performance analysis. *Journal of Marketing, 41*(1), 77–79.

Matzler, K., & Sauerwein, E. (2002). The factor structure of customer satisfaction: An empirical test of the importance grid and the penalty-reward-contrast analysis. *International Journal of Service Industry Management, 13*(4), 314–332.

Parasuraman, A. A. (2004). Assessing and improving service performance for maximum impact: Insights from a two-decade-long research journey. *Performance Measurement and Metrics, 5*(2), 45–52.

Parasuraman, A., Berry, L. L., & Zeithaml, V. A. (1991). Understanding customer expectations of service. *Sloan Management Review, 32*(3), 39–48.

Randall, L., & Senior, M. (1994). A model for achieving quality in hospital hotel services. *International Journal of Contemporary Hospitality Management, 6*(1/2), 68–74.

Severt, D., Wang, Y., Chen, P., & Breiter, D. (2007). Examining the motivation, perceived performance, and behavioral intentions of convention attendees: Evidence from a regional conference. *Tourism Management, 28*, 399–408.

Walker, J., & Baker, J. (2000). An exploratory study of a multi-expectation framework for services. *Journal of Services Marketing, 14*(5), 411–431.

Zeithaml, V A., Berry, L. L., & Parasuraman, A. (1993). The nature and determinants of customer expectations of service. *Journal of the Academy of Marketing Science, 21*(1), 1–12.

CHAPTER 4

LUXURY TOURISTS: CELEBRITIES' PERSPECTIVES

Antónia Correia, Metin Kozak and Helena Reis

ABSTRACT

Luxury tourism is the behaviour of a minority of travellers. Our objective is to assess how Celebrities perceive and experience tourism luxuries. Furthermore, their inner concept of luxury tourism is analysed by comparison with their everyday perception of luxury, and, finally, to understand to what extent luxury relates to outrageous spending. We interviewed 36 Portuguese Celebrities and a group comprising ordinary individuals in order to account for heterogeneity control. A mixed approach of quantitative and qualitative methods was applied in the interpretation of the interviews. The findings reveal diverse perceptions of luxury tourism by the different groups.

Keywords: Luxury tourism; snobbism; social status; conformity; hedonic value; Celebrities

Tourists' Perceptions and Assessments
Advances in Culture, Tourism and Hospitality Research, Volume 8, 43–51
ISSN: 1871-3173/doi:10.1108/S1871-317320140000008011

INTRODUCTION

Luxury consumption and leisure are considered as a privilege of the 'lords of the manor', the privilege of a minority (Veblen, 1899). In contrast, Nicosia (1966) shows that luxury consumption is more of a feature in bourgeois and lower classes than in the wealthier ones (Nicosia, 1966). More recently, Eastman, Goldsmith, and Flynn (1999) argue that luxury leisure and consumption are everywhere and that everyone desires luxuries. The increasing number of contributions in the field of luxury is not so evident on tourism/As far as luxury tourism is concerned, one of the first contributions came from Riley (1995), who argued that luxury in this context is related to attractions and activities or to tourists' actions, skills and attitudes/This means that tourism is also allied with luxury, whether it is by tourists' attitudes or by the destination they visit. In one way or another, to define what luxury tourism is all about is critical to reinforcing this market niche.

This puts the discussion of the sense of luxury tourism consumption on interpersonal and personal levels. In this light that this research arose, first to assess how individuals with a high socio-economic status (the contemporary lavish society – Portuguese Celebrities) perceived tourism luxuries; second, to analyse how they experience luxuries in tourism, since for these individuals, luxury is a feature of the manner of travelling rather than necessarily of the destination they are travelling to; third, to enlighten us on whether their inner concept of luxury tourism differs from their everyday meanings of luxury; and fourth, to understand to what extent luxury relates to outrageous or excessive spending and these individuals' willingness to assume this in an explicit way.

This research uses a snowball convenience sample of 36 Portuguese citizens, 27 of which can be classed as 'Celebrities' (famous and public persons), and the remaining group, which is composed of ordinary individuals introduced here to control the heterogeneity of perceptions and meanings that each group tends to express. In this chapter we test how the different groups perceive luxury tourism both internally and outwardly.

THEORETICAL CONSIDERATIONS

The main values describing luxury consumption, whether relating to products or tourism, are: conformity, snobbism, status and hedonism.

Conformity and snobbism rely on interpersonal influence being conferent of status by peer groups' acceptance or emulation (Mason, 1993). Conformity refers to the behaviours or attitudes that conform to social norms in strict accordance with peer-group membership (Kotler, 1965). Thus, in destination choice, tourists conform to the opinion of their peer groups. Social compliance leads tourists to the same place where the majority of others go or recommend. What Leibenstein (1950) calls the 'bandwagon effect' refers to the desire of people to purchase a commodity in order to conform to the people they wish to be associated with, in order to be fashionable or stylish. In terms of tourism, holidays in popular destinations where many others go are perceived as able to confer the level of compliance tourists seek with their peer groups, relating also to prestige; worthy behaviour that is able to confer status. Snobbism refers to uniqueness and distinctiveness. Tourists that exhibit snobbish behaviour wish to be different and exclusive: differentiating and distancing themselves from the 'common herd' are drivers of their behaviour.

In tourism, experiences out of the ordinary (exclusivity) or unique travel experiences (uniqueness) give tourists a sense of prestige, conferring status through a perceived increase in social standing and impressing others. Both interpersonal values may be regarded as antecedents of a behaviour that is mostly driven by the desire for social status (consequent). Social status refers to the social recognition/uniqueness or the conformity of tourist behaviour that the others may confer to a certain tourist (Kapferer & Bastien, 2009). Grubb and Grathwohl (1967) argue that every person has a self-concept and that they intend to enhance it through the consumption of goods as symbols. Mason (1981, 1984) posits that status pursuit is the most important motive in conspicuous consumption, and it exists across all social classes. Consumers tend to purchase luxuries in order to express personal distinction and establish social identity (Batra, Ramaswamy, Alden, Steenkamp, & Ramachander, 2000).

Hedonic value refers to an essential element that individuals perceive in forming their own hedonic experience. Dubois and Laurent (1996) maintain that an increasing number of consumers purchase luxuries primarily to gratify themselves rather than to impress others. This tendency is more obvious in people with high personal orientation (Vigneron & Johnson, 1999). Hedonic value and social status should be regarded as consequents; while hedonic value refers to the functional value of the consumptions or leisure experiences, social status refers to the social value of these commodities.

METHOD

In order to elicit the most relevant facets of luxury tourism from Portuguese Celebrities and as a result of the exploratory nature of our study, mixed research methods were undertaken. 'Celebrities' are people that exert a significant influence on several facets of society, ranging from arts, music, movies and television, sports, culture, politics, religion and even 'Socialites', who have no defined careers apart from looking beautiful and attending the right events.

According to Fink (1995), snowball sampling is considered the best way to obtain participants for this kind of study. Theoretical sampling considers unique combinations of case profiles across four to seven attributes (Woodside, MacDonald, & Burford, 2005), and recommends five to eight interviews per cell. Hence, through this method 27 Celebrities were interviewed, 9 for each social group, plus an additional 9-person control group, comprising ordinary people to account for heterogeneity. By doing this, we assumed Celebrities perceive tourism differently from ordinary people; moreover, within the Celebrity group, we predicted there would be different perceptions in the various groups (Musicians, Reporters and Socialites). Therefore, we were able to identify four different groups: our sample contains nine Musicians, nine Reporters working in social and fashion magazines and nine Socialites, as well as nine ordinary individuals. Despite the recommendations of McCracken (1988) and Woodside et al. (2005), this sample is representative only of the respondents' behaviour. The interview guide was based on 'a progressive approach' (McCracken, 1988), moving from topic to topic in order not to disorientate respondents (Curwin & Slater, 2002). The first section characterizes the participants' tourism experience.

The second section assesses their tourism-based intentions, whereas the third assesses the concept of luxury in tourism and the most outrageous tourism or social experience interviewees can remember. The fourth section, quantitative in its essence, aims to get participants' overall perceptions of what a luxury tourism experience is. The four perceived values of luxury — conformity, snobbism, social status and hedonic value — were measured with items adapted from previous relevant literature; a five-point Likert scale ranging from 'totally disagree' to 'totally agree' was used in order to test the importance and relevance of tourism luxuries for respondents.

FINDINGS

First, a series of exploratory factor analyses were performed. Then, a composite score was computed for each construct by averaging the items pertaining to the construct. From the 24 items initially considered to measure the four main perceptions of tourism luxury, 13 remained − the ones that are perceived by Portuguese Celebrities (75%) and ordinary individuals (25%) as manifests of tourism luxury values. The box plot shows some heterogeneity in perceptions, suggesting that inter- and intra-group differences exist.

The Musicians on average tended to value snobbism less than conformity, whereas the Reporters presented unusual preferences that emphasized most the hedonic value of their holidays. Almost half of the Reporters tended to perceive holidays as a non-snobbish pursuit while the other half as a non-conformity activity. Socialites are the snobbiest group, their distinctive attitude focusing on gaining social status and pleasure. Surprisingly, it was the group of ordinary people that most valued the status that the holidays may confer on them, whether it was by assuming a snobbish attitude or a conformist one. Qualitative analysis reinforces these results. The interviewees were asked, How do you define a luxury tourism experience? Their answers enlighten us as to what they value the most. In order to enlighten the differences a word cloud (using NVivo10) was designed for each group, as Fig. 1 illustrates, to ensure that differences were sufficiently clear. Some excerpts from the interviews are also included below, describing their perceptions.

For the Portuguese social groups, conformity with family and friends' expectations was the primary motivation for luxury tourism experiences, this being a sign that the social value of tourism prevailed at the time of deciding their holidays. For the 'Musicians', family always came first at the time of choosing their dream holiday. With their companion they aimed to get away from the common social etiquette or code that normally inhibited them in order to have fun without being censored. Furthermore, the destination did not matter as long as they could remain anonymous in a pleasant place where they could have fun with their friends or family. Excerpts from their interviews provide compelling evidence for these conclusions: Any destination, as long as it is with my family and in a place where I won't be recognized.

For this group that is used to dealing with crowds, their preferences while on holiday were focused on being with the family, outside the influences of

Fig. 1. Meaning of Outrageous Holidays by Social Group.

their popularity; unplanned destinations without frills, whereas the 'Reporters' tended to persist in relating luxury with destinations full of history and experiences capable of providing them the hedonic pleasure of learning about other cultures. The Reporters observe: Locations that are politically safe, hot climate, nice beaches.

Socialites relate luxury to holidays paid for by others and reported favouring the travel experiences capable of giving them the sense of social status that drives their lives; therefore parties and social recognition drove their luxury perceptions: Zanzibar, with my girlfriend, at a local logging. I would engage on some sort of photography work and travel writing in order to share it with my friends.

'Ordinary' people, instead, chose to differentiate themselves from the others: experiencing some thrills and adventures in a pleasant and exquisite destination were the most valued perceptions of luxury tourism: Striking, breath-taking scenery, staying at a very comfortable … maybe in a palace, those that are now used as hotels, a destination where I can learn more about different peoples and cultures.

This result, although exploratory in nature, shows quite
ury in tourism has different meanings and that most of these ...
relate to the status and social position people have. Furthermore, there is a
clear tendency to escape from their usual lives, and this has also been identified in other research as being the essence of holidays (Pearce, 2005). The
results show that the more status people have, the less likely it is that their
decision relies on seeking higher status.

CONCLUSION AND IMPLICATIONS

Tourism is somehow allied with luxury, whether it is through tourists' attitudes or through the destination they visit. Riley (1995) posits that luxury
is more in the manner of travelling than in the destination. This was confirmed to some extent in this research, since most of the social groups that
participated in this study reported that the destination was not the most
important attribute. However, according to Correia and Kozak (2012), luxury is also found in selected destinations, and our participants also con-
formed to these authors' proposal, as it was possible to draw overall
conclusions about those destinations perceived to be luxury.

The results evidence that when choosing their own holidays, privacy
drove these Celebrities' decisions, even though they were aware and understood luxury tourism as a way of improving social standing. In fact, luxury
tourism relies on personal values rather than on interpersonal ones, at least
for individuals who deal with fame and status on a daily basis. For them,
luxury is 'to be with their families in quiet and private resorts, where quality and hedonic value prevail', whereas ordinary people perceived luxury as
the most different, exquisite and thrilling tourism experience.

Regarding our second objective: to analyse how they experienced luxuries in tourism, since for these individuals, luxury is in the manner of travelling rather than in the destination they are travelling to, the four groups
show different perceptions. While on holidays, the Musicians, who are
daily in the spotlight, preferred to be with their families, away from the
pressure of their popularity. The Reporters related luxury with historical
and cultural destinations, capable of providing them the hedonic pleasure
of learning about other cultures, customs and civilizations. The Socialites
related luxury to holidays paid for by others and enjoyed travel experiences
that gave them the sense of social status that drives their lives, whereas
ordinary people related luxury to differentiation, a differentiation that

needed to be perceived when they got back home via a number of photos to show to their friends and family. Moreover, the topic of luxury has been regarded with a certain prejudice in general, and Portuguese Celebrities are no exception; the Musicians and Reporters tended to refuse to recognize outrageous spending as a proxy of luxury, while the Socialites and the group of ordinary people did disclose outrageous spending.

Our third proposition: to highlight whether or not their inner concept of luxury tourism differs from the one they accept for their daily lives is also answered. The Musicians on average perceived conformity as very important to devaluating snobbism. Emulation of family and hedonic value drove their desire for a luxury experience. The Reporters focused on hedonic pleasure rather than on social values. Yet for this group, the hedonic value was more related to learning and social knowledge; snobbism or conformity was not so evident. Socialites proved to be the snobbiest group among the Celebrities group, their distinctive attitude to luxury tourism being a way of gaining social status and pleasure. In fact, they associated luxury tourism experiences with being recognized and gaining more popularity. Nevertheless, the snobbiest group overall was that of ordinary people, who tended to relate luxury to exquisite and different experiences.

Our results, exploratory in nature, indicate that the individuals' status and social position expose different meanings of luxury in tourism. Furthermore, the heterogeneity of the perceptions gathered suggests that the lower the social status of individuals, the thirstier they are in searching for this while on holiday. This means that the more status people have, the less likely it is that their decision relies on seeking more status. Moreover, the findings show that there was a clear tendency for the latter to run away from their usual lives, confirming that this is the essence of holidays (Pearce, 2005). Nevertheless, the present research focuses only on Portuguese individuals, which is limited and therefore not generalizable. The need for additional studies is evident to assess the relevance of luxury tourism and consumption among other nationalities, in broader and more diversified groups and within different cultural, social and economic contexts.

REFERENCES

Batra, R., Ramaswamy, V., Alden, D. L., Steenkamp, J. B., & Ramachander, S. (2000). Effects of brand local and nonlocal origin on consumer attitudes in developing countries. *Journal of Consumer Psychology*, *9*(2), 83–95.

Correia, A., & Kozak, M. (2012). Exploring prestige and status on domestic destinations: The case of Algarve. *Annals of Tourism Research, 39,* 1951–1967.

Curwin, J., & Slater, R. (2002). *Quantitative methods for business decision* (5th ed.). London: Thomson Learning.

Dubois, B., & Laurent, G. (1996). The functions of luxury: A situational approach to excursionism. *Advances in Consumer Research, 23,* 470–477.

Eastman, J., Goldsmith, R., & Flynn, L. (1999). Status consumption in consumer behavior: Scale development and validation. *Journal of Marketing Theory and Practice, 7*(2), 41–52.

Fink, A. (1995). *How to measure survey reliability and validity* (Vol. 7). Thousand Oaks, CA: Sage.

Grubb, E. L., & Grathwohl, H. L. (1967). Consumer self-concept, symbolism and market behavior: A theoretical approach. *Journal of Marketing, 31,* 22–27.

Kapferer, J. N., & Bastien, V. (2009). *The luxury strategy.* London: Kogan Page.

Kotler, P. (1965). Behavior models for analyzing buyers. *Journal of Marketing, 29,* 37–45.

Leibenstein, H. (1950). Bandwagon, snob, and Veblen effects in the theory of consumers' demand. *Quarterly Journal of Economics, 64*(May), 183–207.

Mason, R. (1981). *Conspicuous consumption: A study of exceptional consumer behaviour.* New York, NY: St. Martin Press.

Mason, R. (1984). Conspicuous consumption: A literature review. *European Journal of Marketing, 18*(3), 26–39.

Mason, R. (1993). Cross-cultural influences on the demand for status goods, European. *Advances in Consumer Research, 1,* 46–51.

McCracken, G. (1988). *The long interview.* Newbury Park, CA: Sage.

Nicosia, F. M. (1966). *Consumer decision processes.* Englewood Cliffs, NJ: Prentice-Hall.

Pearce, P. (2005). Tourist behaviour: Themes and conceptual schemes. In C. Cooper, C. Hall, & D. Timothy (Eds.), *Aspects of tourism* (Vol. 27). Clevedon: Channel View Publications.

Riley, R. (1995). Prestige worthy tourist behaviour. *Annals of Tourism Research, 22*(3), 630–649.

Veblen, T. (1899). *The theory of the leisure class.* New York, NY: Vanguard Press.

Vigneron, F., & Johnson, L. (1999). A review and a conceptual framework of prestige-seeking consumer behavior. *Academy of Marketing Science Review, 9*(1), 1–14.

Woodside, A. G., MacDonald, R., & Burford, M. (2005). Holistic case-based modelling of customers' thinking-doing destination choice. In R. March & A. G. Woodside (Eds.), *Tourism behavior: Travellers' decisions and actions* (pp. 73–111). Oxon: CABI.

CHAPTER 5

NONTRIVIAL BEHAVIORAL IMPLICATIONS OF TRIVIAL DESIGN CHOICES IN TRAVEL WEBSITES

Eyal Ert

ABSTRACT

The internet is rapidly becoming the main channel for seeking and booking travel services. The consequent human—interface interactions are now the focal point of many studies being conducted by both scholars and practitioners. The development of websites involves many design choices, such as background, colors, fonts, and different ways of presenting information. The study here argues that these seemingly "trivial" design choices may have nontrivial effects on customers' behavior. The study presents three empirical examples supporting this idea. The first example refers to the presentation of hotels as items on a list on websites, which creates a "mere position" effect. The second example shows that different partitioning of an attribute's values can impact their relative

Tourists' Perceptions and Assessments
Advances in Culture, Tourism and Hospitality Research, Volume 8, 53–59
Copyright © 2014 by Emerald Group Publishing Limited
All rights of reproduction in any form reserved
ISSN: 1871-3173/doi:10.1108/S1871-317320140000008002

importance. The third example shows that background features (color, picture) may result in priming effects. In all cases, the seemingly trivial changes in design directly alter customers' choices although, rationally, they should have no impact at all.

Keywords: Internet; e-tourism; e-commerce; choice; e-hospitality; priming

INTRODUCTION

The increasing role of the internet in hospitality and tourism is drawing attention to the importance of website design. The idea that a website's design affects both performance and evaluation of service quality has motivated assessments of "web service quality" and its dimensions (Kim & Lee, 2005), user needs (Chu, 2001), and relative importance of contents (Law & Hsu, 2005). Recent comprehensive reviews of website design frameworks (Hashim, Murphy, & Law, 2007; Ip, Law, & Lee, 2011) have mapped the importance of these and related factors. Those studies have provided useful and applicable insights for website designers to ensure both customer performance and a positive evaluation of the relevant services on the web.

In addition to these factors, website designers also have to make frequent arbitrary design choices, such as choosing among different formats to present information (e.g., items presented in a list, rows, or tables), and selecting colors, backgrounds, and fonts. In the current chapter I argue that while these choices may seem trivial, they might have nontrivial effects, warranting more in-depth study of these effects by both scholars and practitioners. To support this claim, I present three empirical examples demonstrating surprising effects of trivial design choices: the consequence of presenting items in a list which creates "mere position effects," the consequence of presenting attributes in categories that might create "partitioning effects," and the consequence of using certain backgrounds which might create "priming effects." Each of these examples demonstrates how even trivial (supposedly neutral) design choices directly affect the customer's decision-making process and may alter his or her choices. I briefly explain the suggested psychological mechanism behind each effect, and discuss their implications for both research and practice.

PRESENTING ITEMS IN LISTS AND THE "MERE POSITION" EFFECT

Many online travel agent (OTA) websites present hotels or flights in lists. This design seems a trivial way of presenting information, yet it implies that hotels listed online now have a new attribute: their position on the list. Research on consumer psychology shows that although this attribute is spurious, it might actually affect customer choice. For example, Dayan and Bar-Hillel (2011) demonstrated that the position of food items on a restaurant's menu affects their likelihood of being chosen.

Ert and Fleishcer (2013) tested the potential of this mere position effect in the context of booking hotels online. They conducted an online experiment in which they asked 858 participants to book a hotel in Tel Aviv using a website that was specifically created for the experiment. The website presented 10 (real) hotels with similar attributes to choose from, and it was designed like a typical OTA website. The participants were randomly assigned to 1 of 10 experimental conditions, in which the hotels' order on the list was manipulated. Thus, across conditions, each hotel appeared at least once in each position on the list.

The results revealed a significant mere position effect: the observed-choice proportions for each position on the list were significantly different from 10% (the rate expected under uniform preferences), $\chi^2(9, N=856)=42.22$, $p < 0.0001$. The choice rates followed a U-shaped trend, such that when hotels were listed in the first three positions they were most likely to be selected (likelihood of 12.8, 13.1, and 12.7%, respectively), hotels positioned at the end of the list also received values higher than 10%, whereas hotels positioned as 5th and 6th on the list were the least likely to be selected (6 and 6.6%, respectively). A mixed logit analysis confirmed the significance of this choice trend, even when other hotel attributes, such as price and review score, were controlled for (for details see Ert & Fleischer, 2013).

Note that although the experiment focuses on booking hotels, the results might be relevant to any item that is presented in a list format online. In the tourism industry, relevant items include lodging facilities, flights, and attractions. These findings are also likely to be relevant not only for choice between services, but also for choice between different attributes of the same service. For example, position might affect the choice between different types of rooms offered by a hotel on its own website. This "primacy-recency" pattern is well known in psychology, and was first observed in studies assessing memory recall of items presented consecutively

(Deese & Kaufman, 1957). In the context of item evaluation online, the evidence suggests that first and last items are not only more likely to be recalled, but also seem to receive greater attention when the list is being scanned for information. Overall, Ert and Fleischer's study showed that although the hotel's position on the list is a spurious attribute, it affects traveler decisions and as such, should not be overlooked.

GROUPING AND PARTITIONING SERVICE ATTRIBUTES AND THE "DIVERSIFICATION BIAS"

Another relevant design choice of web developers, which also relates to information presentation, addresses the presentation format for a service's different attributes (Martin & Norton, 2009). The same attributes may be grouped into one category (e.g., "room cleanliness and comfort") or presented separately ("room cleanliness," "room comfort"). Martin and Norton (2009) show that the latter presentation increases the weight customers assign to the category and consequently alters their choice. In one of the experiments they asked participants to choose 1 out of 10 hotel options based on a 5-point scale rating for each of the categories displayed. Half of the hotels were ranked higher on room attributes (cleanliness and comfort), while the others were ranked higher on hotel attributes (service and conditions). The results showed that the preference for hotels with the better rooms was much higher when the room attributes were presented separately (98% of choice) than when they were grouped into the same category (80%). The behavioral regularity that seems to underlie this effect is people's tendency to spread consumption evenly across categories of options, exhibiting a "diversification bias" (Read & Loewenstein, 1995). This tendency applies to any categorization of items, and thus it applies to both categorizing products, services, and tourist activities (Kahn & Ratner, 2005), and categorizing attributes (as in the current example).

PAGE BACKGROUND AND THE EFFECT OF "VISUAL PRIMES"

The first two examples, demonstrating how trivial web-design choices influence customer behavior, referred to the form of information presentation.

What about design choices that are not directly related to the way information is presented? Can a webpage's graphical background, for example, influence the service one buys? A series of experiments performed by Mandel and Johnson (2002) suggest that it might. One way in which background might shape behavior is by affecting implicit memory, an effect called "priming." The idea is that exposure to a certain stimulus, the "prime," increases accessibility to information that already exists in one's memory and often causes this information to be incorporated into subsequent judgments and actions.

In one of Mandel and Johnson's (2002) experiments, participants were first presented with a "welcome page" that contained information on a hypothetical shopping site. The background for this page was either blue with clouds (to prime comfort) or green with pennies (to prime price). The participant then moved on to the "product webpage" featuring two sofas which they were asked to choose from: the "Palisades," an economical but less comfortable sofa, and the "Knightbridge," which was more comfortable but expensive. The results showed that the more comfortable and expensive sofa had a market share of 61% among those primed with comfort (blue background with clouds), while its market share dropped to only 44% among those who were primed with price (green background with pennies). Interestingly, none of the participants, in either group, were aware of these effects.

CONCLUSION AND IMPLICATIONS

The endless design possibilities for contemporary website designers suggest that the three examples presented herein represent only a few cases in a much larger set of potential nontrivial effects of trivial design choices. The psychological effects of colors, for example, are well known to psychologists and have been much studied for decades. Colors affect product evaluation, mood and performance, as well as perceptions of the environment (store, website; see, e.g., Bellizzi, Crowley, & Hasty, 1983). Even the choice of fonts might result in nontrivial effects. For example, recent studies suggest that people might perceive things that are "hard to read" as things that are "hard to do" (Song & Schwarz, 2008). In one study, participants read the recipe for a Japanese roll; it was found that when the recipe was written in a "hard to read" font (Mistral, 12), participants rated the skills of the restaurant's chef as higher than when the dish was described in an "easy to read" font (Ariel, 12) (5.2 and 4.1, respectively, on a 7-point rating scale).

These few examples suggest that nontrivial consequences of "trivial design choices" may be applicable to a large range of businesses, as they affect the perception of services and places, and might alter choice behavior between services and/or between their offerings. As such, to really understand online behavior we should further investigate the relevance, potential magnitude of impact, and boundaries of these effects.

ACKNOWLEDGMENT

The topic and the contents of this chapter were inspired by the discussions, comments, and helpful advice I received from the participants of the 8th Consumer Psychology of Tourism, Hospitality, and Leisure (CPTHL) Symposium, Istanbul, 2013.

REFERENCES

Bellizzi, J. A., Crowley, A. E., & Hasty, R. W. (1983). The effects of color in store design. *Journal of Retailing, 59*, 21–45.

Chu, R. (2001). What online Hong Kong travelers look for on airline/travel websites? *International Journal of Hospitality Management, 20*, 95–100.

Dayan, E., & Bar-Hillel, M. (2011). Nudge to nobesity II: Menu positions influence food orders. *Judgment and Decision Making, 6*, 333–342.

Deese, J., & Kaufman, R. A. (1957). Serial effects in recall of unorganized and sequentially organized verbal material. *Journal of Experimental Psychology, 54*, 180.

Ert, E., & Fleischer, A. (2013). *Position effects in online hotel booking.* Manuscript under review.

Hashim, N. H., Murphy, J., & Law, R. (2007). A review of hospitality website design frameworks. In M. Sigala, L. Mich, & J. Murphy (Eds.), *Information and communication technologies in tourism 2007* (pp. 219–230). New York, NY: Springer.

Ip, C., Law, R., & Lee, H. A. (2011). A review of website evaluation studies in the tourism and hospitality fields from 1996 to 2009. *International Journal of Tourism Research, 13*, 234–265.

Kahn, B. E., & Ratner, R. K. (2005). Variety for the sake of variety? Diversification motives in consumer choice. In S. Ratneshwar & D. Mick (Eds.), *Inside consumption: frontiers of research on consumer motives, goals, and desires* (pp. 102–121). New York, NY: Routledge.

Kim, W. G., & Lee, H. Y. (2005). Comparison of web service quality between online travel agencies and online travel suppliers. *Journal of Travel & Tourism Marketing, 17*, 105–116.

Law, R., & Hsu, C. H. C. (2005). Customers' perceptions on the importance of hotel web site dimensions and attributes. *International Journal of Contemporary Hospitality Management, 17*, 493–503.

Mandel, N., & Johnson, E. J. (2002). When web pages influence choice: Effects of visual primes on experts and novices. *Journal of Consumer Research, 29*, 235–245.

Martin, J. M., & Norton, M. I. (2009). Shaping online consumer choice by partitioning the web. *Psychology & Marketing, 26*, 908–926.

Read, D., & Loewenstein, G. (1995). Diversification bias: Explaining the discrepancy in variety seeking between combined and separated choices. *Journal of Experimental Psychology, 1*, 34.

Song, H., & Schwarz, N. (2008). If it's hard to read, it's hard to do: Processing fluency affects effort prediction and motivation. *Psychological Science, 19*, 986–988.

CHAPTER 6

THE ROLE OF SOCIAL PSYCHOLOGY IN THE TOURISM EXPERIENCE MODEL (TEM)

Juergen Gnoth

ABSTRACT

The tourism experience model (TEM) is a meta-analytical, phenomen-ological inspired model of how tourists experience destinations. This essay argues that social and cultural psychology form only part of the analysis of how the tourist's consciousness filters interactions. By con-sidering the existential self versus the role-authentic self of social psy-chology, the TEM adds to social psychology's scope explaining how and why tourists may experience social interactions. In addition, it models the dynamics of how the tourist experiences his own activity (exploratory vs. recreational). The model thereby goes beyond both the exclusive social focus and the ego-centric notion of the Individualism−Collectivism dichotomy.

Keywords: Experience; socio-cultural psychology; existentialism; Individualism; Collectivism

Tourists' Perceptions and Assessments
Advances in Culture, Tourism and Hospitality Research, Volume 8, 61−69
Copyright © 2014 by Emerald Group Publishing Limited
All rights of reproduction in any form reserved
ISSN: 1871-3173/doi:10.1108/S1871-317320140000008003

INTRODUCTION

The TEM is a meta-analytical, phenomenological inspired model of how tourists experience destinations. TEM represents a view on how we may research and gain insight into tourists' being-in-the-world (Heidegger, 1927). During the discussion of this model at the CPTHL in Istanbul, Turkey (1–5 June 2013), a comment by an engaged participant triggered the creation of this essay. The critique questioned the extent to which this model was offering anything new as social psychology appears to be covering its ground already.

This essay argues that while naturally overlaps occur with that discipline, the TEM covers additional ground. In particular, it is a model that seeks to understand the individual's lived experience (Husserl, 1912) and argues that this experience provides the platform, not the consequence for socio-psychological concepts to find application. In other words, the tourist's experience takes precedence and, ultimately, poses as the arbiter to suggest how and which socio-psychological concepts such as values or Individualism versus Collectivism apply (e.g. Hofstede, 1984; Schwartz, 1992; Triandis, 1994).

Comprised of two foundational axes – Activities and Consciousness, the TEM permits researchers to describe the process of experiencing at the systems level (see Fig. 1). The first axis or dimension represents a psychic system's activities as either, repetitive, recreating and consolidating, or as exploratory. To maintain itself and to survive, every living system needs to accomplish two basic sets of processes. The first involves continuous, self-reflective restoration, reinvention and consolidation of practice and of the self (Bourdieu, 1986); the second involves the activities that are exploratory, testing, experimental and learning, as each system needs to grow or change in order to adapt. Hence, the repetitive and consolidating activities relate to a system's being while the exploratory activities relate to a system's becoming including growth and learning.

The second axis or dimension comprises an individual's spectrum of options by which his or her consciousness perceives its own activities, that is how awareness perceives and filters the information received via the senses. The poles of this axis indicate whether the mind receives its activities either as more role-authentic, on one hand or more existentially authentic on the other. Role authenticity, in this case, describes the level to which the mind evaluates its activity with socially acquired norms, values and expectations, or to which it views it as existentially authentic, that is,

The Tourism Experience Model

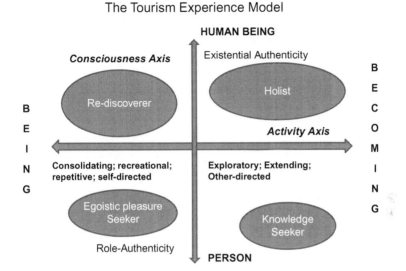

Fig. 1. The Tourism Experience Model. *Source:* Adapted from Gnoth and Deans (n.d.).

humanistically determined by the extent to which activities create convergence between situation and felt emotions (e.g. sharing resources between benevolent and friendly strangers). Existential authenticity is both the feeling and awareness of oneness with one's environment.

Hence, when positioning an individual's awareness at the centre of deliberations, socio-psychological and anthropological models (e.g. Adamopoulos & Kashima, 1999; Schwartz, 1992; Triandis, 1994) can be applied to the TEM's spectrum of how the self actually experiences the physical and social environment. The socially generated tools and mechanisms by which the individual perceives, understands and acts in the world (e.g. language and habitus) are necessarily directed towards the environment, society and specific others. However, the TEM focuses on how the self — and whatever particular conceptualisation or focal configuration of this self, then achieves (self-)realisation. Such an application would further highlight the experiential qualities of the socio-psychological conceptualisations of the Individualism—Collectivism dichotomy as much as those of values which are understood as beliefs of preferred conduct or end states (Hofstede, 1984; Schwartz, 1992; Triandis, 1994).

THE RELATIONSHIP BETWEEN THE TEM AND SOCIAL PSYCHOLOGY

Historically, social psychology is a relative newcomer to the modern social sciences as founded by Comte (1798–1857). The interactions between individual and society have been subject to philosophical and strategic deliberations of particularly rulers and their educators since time immemorial. In other words, after the decline of solitary hunting societies and since social stratification and the organisation of cultures took hold (Adamopoulos & Kashima, 1999; Triandis, 1988) the need for reflecting on social conduct and control began to emerge. A quick glance at the world-wide web shows that

> Social psychology is about understanding individual behavior in a social context. McLeod (2007, p. 6) further cites, Baron, Byrne, and Suls (1989), '*Who define* social psychology *as* "the scientific field that seeks to understand the nature and causes of individual behavior in social situations"'. It looks at human behavior as influenced by other people and the social context in which this occurs. Social psychologists therefore deal with the factors that lead us to behave in a given way in the presence of others, and look at the conditions under which certain behavior/actions and feelings occur. Social psychology is to do with the way these feelings, thoughts, beliefs, intentions and goals are constructed and how such psychological factors, in turn, influence our interactions with others. (Saul McLeod, 2007)

Clearly, the focus of concern is the social environment. Although psychology informs this discipline with key concepts – such as dissonance (Festinger, 1957) that indicates a feeling of unbalance, or attitude (Fishbein & Ajzen, 1975) indicating a like or dislike, and intentionality, researchers view them mostly as socio-psychological determinants in relation to their target as both these concepts' affective and cognitive elements often coincide with socially learned or socially oriented contexts. This contrasts with the TEM insofar as it not only describes a state or 'being' but it also describes how we can conceive of the individual's 'becoming' or the process by which the social or any other environment is explored. In fact, the TEM helps further determine why and how an individual acts as a person and why and how as an individual. The Individualism–Collectivism dichotomy then helps in the classification of whether the activity can be considered collectivistic versus individualistic.

According to Fisher (1982, p. 7), the first textbook in social psychology was written by Ross (1908) followed by McDougall (1908). Fisher also maintains that 'due to so much independence and separation (of conceptual developments and as the discipline emerged) it is now accurate to speak of two schools of social psychology: "psychological social psychologists" emphasise the functioning of the individual; "sociological social psychologists" emphasise the functioning of the social system in which the individual is embedded'. Yet he continues that the emphasis of the methodology used by both is the study of human social behaviour.

In a similar manner, Schubert and Klein (2011) maintain that social psychology as a social science studies the influence of social groups on the individual and the consequences of this relationship on the social order. Both the above American as well as the German sources emphasise that one of the major drivers for the development of the discipline of social psychology was the rapid changes that occurred during the aftermath of the industrial revolution, the two World Wars, and include issues such as racism and gender issues.

For the TEM, which focuses on how the tourist actually experiences holidays, social psychology is of particular importance when seeking an understanding of how experiencing interacts with and is influenced by both the social home-environment and the learning that takes place there vis-à-vis the host environment. However, in addition, the inclusion of the existential sphere of experiencing addresses the outcome for the individual (as opposed to the person) over and above his or her own impact on the social environment as ascertained by others, including sociologists. As Fisher notes in his introduction the role of social psychology is particularly to understand and enhance social life; the TEM further includes the individual's possibilities and ways for achieving self-realisation within and outside this social life (see Maslow, 1964). The TEM thus seeks to distinguish between what an individual does and how they experience as persons (which always implies an observer, including how oneself thinks how others see them, see also Luhmann, 1995), versus how they experience as individuals. Such an existential understanding of the self goes beyond the egocentric self implied in the Individualism—Collectivism dichotomy touted in social anthropology.

As Adamopoulos and Kashima inform us the individualistic orientation such as the one the TEM deals with is a relatively new phenomenon. It reflects the individual's increasing awareness about his/her 'self as agent of action and dispositional (as opposed to situational) self-attribution' (1999, p. 65). Citing Triandis (1990) these authors further concur that this self-orientation has come about as a consequence of increasing societal affluence and life's consequent relative predictability and security. Adamopoulos and Kashima (1999) proceed to develop a structural model of Individualism—Collectivism and position it within the context of models by Triandis but also those by Schwartz and Hofstede, all of whom focus on this analytic dichotomy.

In particular, in their structural model of Individualism versus Collectivism, Adamopoulos and Kashima (1999) focus on the central and recurring facets or dimensions of social behaviour. They distinguish between action-orientation (self vs. other), actor-target orientation (general vs. specific), resource exchange type (material vs. symbolic), and between prototypical behaviour patterns including, the concern with individual survival versus narcissism, and self-esteem and self-reliance versus competition, for the general versus specific orientation of the self. The latter forms the content of Individualism. In contrast, for Collectivism, specific behavioural patterns comprise the focus on cooperation and concern with relationships versus conformity and concern with group cohesion for specific other-oriented actions, whereas the concern with societal values and ethnocentrism versus philanthropy is the pattern of general, *other*-oriented behaviour. These authors then proceed to merge their structural model with Schwartz' (1992) circumplex comprising the 10 value dimensions he identifies in his cross-cultural research, and remind us that the circumplex itself also contrasts individualistic and collectivistic value dimensions (e.g. hedonism or achievement vs. conformity or tradition). In other words, these authors view their own elaborations of the Individualism—Collectivism dichotomy as converging with Schwartz' value system.

The TEM adds an experiential and a dynamic component to these models. Clearly, the TEM focuses on the tourist's self (including individualistic, social and/or collectivistic selves) as well as the type of activity s/he sees him/herself as being involved in. For example, let us take Schwartz' dimension of self-transcendence which comprises values that promote understanding, tolerance and welfare of people and nature. Related to the Consciousness dimension we could ask: to what extent does the tourist's behavioural aim conform to socially expected role-behaviours, or how representative is it of the tourist's existentially authentic behaviour. As a short answer, one might highlight that the social, role-conforming desirability of tolerance may be evaluated and judged differently from the individual's goals and ability to experience situations without prejudice.

Related to the activity dimension we could then further ask, is the tourist familiar with that behaviour, or is it a new or exploratory application? If familiar, is the expression of tolerance habitual and automatic in the sense of mindless acceptance, or is it engaged and seeking the re-establishment of previously experienced conditions? In relation to Schwartz' value we could then proceed to ask, to what extent is that behaviour indeed reflective of the values comprised in self-transcendence? This line of questioning is likely to reveal that some tourists' activities promote such values more than others, including the nature of processing in terms of either, a mindless replication of habits (pleasure-seeker), a contrasting experience of difference (knowledge-seeker), an engaged recreation of previously known conditions (rediscoverer) or an open-minded, involved, focused but selfless engagement with the (social) touristic environment. We may also find that these varying types of activities as indicated in Fig. 1 require or teach a certain type of consciousness and may hence determine the benefits of the experience for destination and tourist. The phenomenological organisation of the tourism literature according to the TEM as the focus of the presentation at the CPTHL precisely sought to further substantiate that relationship. The model thereby also highlights that for certain values to become part of truly held beliefs and tools for self-realisation they can only be achieved with certain types of activities and an involved consciousness rather than by merely copying a practiced behaviour as part of people's habitus (Bourdieu, 1986).

This differentiation between the (automatic or conditioned) pursuit of role-behaviour versus existentially held beliefs that help define a self in terms of individual uniqueness rather than a personality typology appears as an understudied aspect in the Individualism–Collectivism yet this may well be the nature of the discipline as previously defined. Nevertheless, the existential self goes beyond the ego-centric understanding of self and, similar to Collectivism, seeks harmony but not through conformity – as a social value, but through convergence of emotions and situation as in the experience of flow (Chikszentmihalyi, 1992) or cognitively, in moments of insight or peak experiences (Maslow, 1964).

CONCLUSION AND IMPLICATIONS

Socio-psychology focuses on the interactions between the person and society and while this includes an individual's affective and cognitive dealings with their social environment, the TEM ('Tourism Experience Model') seeks an understanding of how the individual actually experiences any interactions, whether within social, natural or introspective environments. Although the description and analysis of such experiencing can gain further depth by utilising concepts and constructs of social and cultural psychology, the discussion has highlighted that the TEM also includes the existential self which, historically, is said to emerge as part of ongoing individualisation. By highlighting how an individual may be experiencing his environment as a function of consciousness and activity, the TEM can show if and how the experience consolidates, recreates or rediscovers previously made experiences, or whether the individual is involved in learning and exploration.

The TEM thereby focuses on the dynamics of experiencing itself and discerns whether behaviour serves the individual's being or his/her becoming. Both dimensions of being and becoming thus give further information on both, individual but also societal and even cultural developments: depending on the extent to which new and exploratory behaviour mark a tendency, they amount to a 'becoming' of new states that may or may not introduce new or reinforce commonly held values for individuals and society. In this way the TEM becomes relevant for social psychology while being reliant on the latter for its own construction.

REFERENCES

Adamopoulos, J., & Kashima, Y. (1999). *Social psychology and cultural context.* Thousand Oaks, CA: Sage.

Bourdieu, P. (1986). The forms of social capital. In J. Richardson (Ed.), *Handbook of theory and research for the sociology of education* (pp. 241–248). New York, NY: Greenwood Press.

Chikszentmihalyi, I. S. (1992). *Optimal experience: Psychological studies of flow in consciousness.* Cambridge: Cambridge University Press.

Festinger, L. (1957). *A theory of cognitive dissonance.* Evanston, IL: Row, Peterson.

Fishbein, M., & Ajzen, I. (1975). *Belief, attitude, intention and behavior: An introduction to theory and research.* Reading, MA: Addison-Wesley.

Fisher, R. J. (1982). *Social psychology: An applied approach.* New York, NY: St. Martin's Press.

Gnoth, J., & Deans, K. (n.d.). *Developing the tourism experience model.* Retrieved from http://anzmac.org/conference/2012/papers/532ANZMACFINAL.pdf. Accessed on 16 February 2014.

Heidegger, M. (1927). *Sein und zeit (Being and time).* Tuebingen: Max Niemeyer Verlag.

Hofstede, G. (1984). *Culture's consequences: International differences in work-related values.* Beverly Hills, CA: Sage.

Husserl, E. (1912/1989). Ideen zu einer reinen Phänomenologie und phänomenologischen Philosophie. Zweites Buch. Phänomenologische Untersuchungen zur Konstitution [1912]. Marly Biemel (Ed.). Husserliana 4. Den Haag: Martinus Nijhoff, 1952; Ideas pertaining to a pure phenomenology and to a phenomenological philosophy. *Second book. Studies in the phenomenology of constitution* (R. Rojcewicz & A. Schuwer, Trans.). Dordrecht: Kluwer Academic Publishers.

Luhmann, N. (1995). *Social systems*. Stanford: Stanford University Press.

Maslow, A. H. (1964). *Peak-experiences*. Cleveland, OH: State University of Ohio.

McDougall, W. (1908). *Social psychology*. New York, NY: Luce & Co.

McLeod, S. (2007). *Social psychology*. Retrieved from http://www.simplypsychology.org/social-psychology.html. Accessed on August 20, 2013.

Ross, E. A. (1908). *Social psychology: An outline and source book*. New York, NY: The MacMillan Company.

Schwartz, S. H. (1992). Universals in the content and structure of values: Theoretical advances and empirical tests in 20 countries. *Advances in Experimental Social Psychology, 25*(1), 1−65.

Schubert, K., & Klein, M. (2011). Das Politiklexikon. 5., aktual. Aufl. Bonn: Dietz. Lizenzausgabe Bonn: Bundeszentrale für politische Bildung.

Triandis, H. (1988). Collectivism vs. individualism: A reconceptualization of a basic concept in cross-cultural psychology. In G. K. Verma & C. Bagely (Eds.), *Cross-cultural studies of personality, attitudes and cognition* (pp. 60−95). London: MacMillan.

Triandis, H. C. (1990). Cross-cultural studies of individualism and collectivism. *Nebraska symposium on motivation, 1989*. Lincoln, NE: University of Nebraska Press.

Triandis, H. C. (1994). *Culture and social behavior*. New York, NY: McGraw-Hill Book Company.

CHAPTER 7

ASSESSING NATIONAL DESTINATION-BRANDING TRANSFORMATIONS: THEORY AND APPLICATION TO COSTA RICA'S NATURE-BASED AND MEDICAL TOURISM PRODUCT-SERVICES

Rodrigo Murillo

ABSTRACT

This chapter analyzes the tourism industry from national and regional perspectives, in order to understand the past and current trends in Costa Rica's positioning and branding attributes and strategies for tourism development. The intent here is not to provide an exhaustive comprehensive literature review of academic research on country branding; and so it is by all means a case study as it describes the evolution of the tourism industry in Costa Rica — including the transformative stages the country went through since the 1980s — as planned tourism national management

Tourists' Perceptions and Assessments
Advances in Culture, Tourism and Hospitality Research, Volume 8, 71–109
ISSN: 1871-3173/doi:10.1108/S1871-317320140000008004

programs evolved toward reaching the target of creating a nature-based tourism brand. The medical industry and then medical tourism industries are analyzed in a global basis and the US market is examined in detail because of its potential to develop a new complementary niche for Costa Rica's tourism industry. The chapter intends to asses Costa Rica's potential to become a country brand in medical tourism, leveraged on its natural tourism destination branding status quo.

Keywords: Country branding; Costa Rica; medical tourism; national tourism management; tourism industry cluster

INTRODUCTION

The concept of nation or country branding, also referred as destination branding (Morgan, Pritchard, & Pride, 2002), has become a priority focus for tourism governmental and private agencies. This perspective is not coincidental. According to Baudrillard (1968) in the current semiotic society, signs, symbols and images provide its meaning to consumption of tourism experiences and services; and therefore brands are ideal means to transmit those signs, symbols and images going beyond their original function of distinguishing and identifying; and additionally acquiring a fetishistic qualities of image and power role, as advertisers craft "associations, attributes and characterizations designed to induce psychological responses" (Donald & Gammack, 2007, p. 46). Thus, the challenge for tourism governmental and private agencies is to be able to recognize the unique characteristic of a country or destination in order to develop projects where place-brand image can be leveraged upon those particularities and/or identities.

In Costa Rica many factors have been combined to historically place the nation in a privileged position within Latin America and the region. For instance, currently Costa Rica has one of the highest rankings in the Americas on the Human Development Index (HDI of 0.83), fourth place in Latin-American — below Argentina, Chile, and Uruguay (United Nations Development Program, 2009). Access to drinking water and improved sanitation, overall, is more than 97% and 95%, respectively (World Health Organization, 2012). In 2009, life expectancy at birth was 77 years for males and 81 years females with an average of 79 years, with an average probability of reaching 82 in males, 85 in females and 83 in both sexes (*ibid.*, 2010). The number of deaths under 5 years is 10 per 1,000 live births between 1990 and 2010 (*ibid.*, 2010).

Costa Rica's positioning is one of the most prominent "natural greenest tourist destinations" in the world (Skyscanner, 2009), which makes plausible a reasonable market growth in the near future. Since late 1980s, Costa Rica has developed an image positioning strategy supported by governmental agencies, in particular the Costa Rican Tourism Board (ICT), to the extent that nation has created already a "country brand" especially because of the country's nature attributes. The fact is that the country was ranked 25th in 2012 and 24th in 2011 according to the Country Brand Index (Future Brand, 2012), being the only country in Latin America to be included in the ranking, in special because of its nature endowments.

The traditional Costa Rican tourism configuration of attributes includes great kindness of the average citizen toward visitors, peaceful environment, natural protection commitment, relative proximity to the largest worldwide outbound tourism markets: Canada and United States (Inman, Mesa, Flores, & Prado, 2002), which may be the main factors that buttress the country's place-brand image.

Costa Rica's natural tourism brand image may be both a competitive and comparative advantage in the tourism industry, setting benchmarks for other countries still on the same path, trying to emulate Costa Rica's recognition as an international destination brand. This is especially noticeable in Central America, where the tourist industry has become one of the major developing and wealth creation mechanisms. For instance, although Costa Rica has historically been the leader in the tourism industry in Central America, in recent years Panama has been the growth frontrunner. According to Blanke, Chiesa, and Crotti (2013) and Blanke and Chiesa (2011), Panama's Travel and Tourism Competiveness Index (TTCI) moved to position 4th within the Central America's region from position 8th in 2011 and jumped to position 37th from position 56th in 2011 and 55th in 2009 in the worldwide ranking. In fact, circa 2009, just after the world's financial collapse, a report from the United Nations World Tourism Organization (UNWTO, 2009, p. 3) published that by Jan/Feb 2009 Panama had already experienced a 7% monthly growth in tourist inbounds, one of the only eight countries worldwide – Lebanon (54%), Morocco (8%), South Africa (6%), Korea (24%), Mexico (13%), Colombia (7%), Chile (6%) were the remaining countries – exhibiting positive growth figures. In comparison, Costa Rica, after being number 42th in 2009 and number 44th in 2011, stepped down to the overall 47th

position by 2013. In the regional ranking Costa Rica ranked 6th after ranking number 5th in 2011.

Nature-based tourism according to Valentine (1992, p. 5), should be limited to the kind of tourism based upon visiting relatively undisturbed natural areas; non-damaging and non-degrading; direct contributor to the
continued protection and management of areas used; and subject to an adequate and appropriate management regime. Activities range from active to
passive, including hiking, adventure tourism, sightseeing, scenic driving,
beach experiences and wildlife viewing (bird watching), where the visitor
combines several experiences in one trip. Nature-based experiences in addition are closely related to all other aspects, such as food, culture, relaxa-
tion, health, accommodation, transport, as they complement each other
and from visitor's overall satisfaction basis.

Thus, identified niches within nature tourism are Soft Adventure
Tourism (moderate physical requirements), Hard adventure tourism (physically demanding and risky), special interest and wildlife tourism (bird
watching – terrestrial or whale watching – marine) and Ecotourism, where
the latter is a tourist experience of natural surroundings supported by principles of sustainability as regards environmental impact and well-being provision to the locals (Wood, 2002). Within the ecotourism niche there is a
sub-niche identified as Scientific Tourism focused on the contribution to
science by means of in situ research, which avoids altering the natural
environment as it is carried out both individually or in small groups.

As Butler (1993, p. 29) proposes, sustainable tourism the sort of tourism
which is "developed and maintained in an area (community, environment)
in such a manner and at such a scale that it remains viable over an infinite
period and does not degrade or alter the environments (human or physical)
in which it exists to such a degree that it prohibits the successful development and well-being of other activities and processes."

Costa Rica historically maintains a competitive position around a wide
concept of sustainable tourism, mainly focused on the three main traditional market segments: ecotourism, sun/beach tourism and adventure
tourism, which combined allow taking advantage of related synergies and
so, offering related tourist products based on natural environment experiences; which in turn strengthens and complements the Costa Rica's country
image.

Although both, private and public sectors in Costa Rica, agree on the
importance of maintaining a nature/conservation based position (Inman
et al., 2002), the drawbacks of massive tourism attraction become sometimes
a tension creator for the sector, as it is thought that an unusual inflow of

visitors could potentially ruin Costa Rica's natural wealth. Medical tourists spend in average six times more than nature-based tourists (Little, 2010), thus, supporting the emergence of the medical tourism industry in Costa Rica could be a logic implementable national strategy to exchange number of visitors for a higher expenditure per capita, without sacrificing the total tourism revenue inflow, and on the contrary potentially increasing it.

Thereby, accurately describing the medical tourism industry in Costa Rica is paramount for identifying competitive advantage factors that could support its further development during the first half of the 21st century. The emergence of a medical-tourism service industry cluster and its associated network is already rooted in Costa Rica, a "sine quo non" requirement toward reaching a final goal: the evolution of a medical tourism industry, as it slowly leaves its incubating stage, targeting to potentially become destination brand in medical tourism as the nation already is in nature-based tourism.

The existing nature-based tourism cluster, as all public and private national players have evolved during the past 30 years, have accumulated a priceless know-how, in terms of both tacit and explicit knowledge, related to designing, launching, marketing, and commercializing nature-based tourism products. The thesis behind this chapter is that Costa Rica can capitalize on this knowledge and develop other related and more sophisticated tourism products-services, such as medical tourism, transforming the country in a destination brand as it has previously done with natural tourism.

EVOLUTION OF TOURISM IN COSTA RICA

Since 1988, the tourism industry has grown more than 600% at a Compound Average Growth Rate (CAGR) of 10%, doubling the average growth rate of the world's aggregated rate figure. The fact and the matter is this trend has only been broken in 1996 and 2001, which makes supposed the industry's life cycle has still a growing trend (Instituto Costarricense de Turismo, 2010). According to JICA and ICT (2001) Costa Rica's tourist industry evolution has gone through three stages since the mid-1980s.

The industry's pioneer phase began as the direct result of catering the ecotourism niche during the 1980s, with a particular focus on scientific tourism. Costa Rica started to differentiate itself by taking advantage of a historic peaceful environmental and political stability, during a period of time when its Central American neighbors were engaged in civil wars.

The country's international image skyrocketed in 1987 when President Arias Sanchez was awarded the Nobel Peace Prize due to his unconditional mediation to terminate the mentioned civil wars, an so, positioning Costa Rica as a "Garden of Peace" in the middle of the Americas (Artavia, Barahona, & Sánchez, 1996). This historic milestone became an international awareness pillar for the country, settings the foundations for the future creation of a Costa Rican brand in tourism, when a set of differentiating factors/elements were internationally projected as part of a public/private initiative to promote Costa Rica as a world class tourist destination. See Table 1 for characteristics of the three stages.

Subsequently, from late 1980s to mid-1990s, the ecotourism lured new market segments with more generic expectations, whose basic objective was simple to enjoy vacations in a natural place, characteristic of the growth phase, heavily based on the massive sun/beach tourism This sort of tourism takes place in coastlines, where the climatic conditions are sunny with mild temperatures (ranging from 25°C to 30°C), allowing tourists to usually sun bath during the day and attend leisure activities during the night. Those tourists usually come from places where beaches are far away and the weather is usually rainy or cloudy most of the year, with low temperature patterns. Sun/beach tourism is an example of mass tourism; normally less demanding and less specialized when compared to more exclusive tourism.

As the industry evolved in the last half of the 1990s decade, changes in visitor's profile evolved: genuine, flexible, more experienced, more demanding and better informed tourists started to arrive, and so, in order to adjust to those specific requirements, the private sector also responded by adjusting the supply side, pushing the emergence of specialized niches, characteristic of the evolution phase.

Although still projecting a strong interest in natural tourism, the market perception was multifaceted including distinct product-services involving sun/beach tourism; meetings, incentives, conferences, and exhibitions (MICE); and intercultural tourism. Sun/beach tourism includes both soft adventure tourism (hiking, mountain biking/bicycling, camping, horseback riding, walking tours, wildlife spotting, whale watching, river and lake canoeing and fishing.) or hard adventure tourism (caving, scuba diving, trekking, white water rafting, kayaking, rock and mountain climbing, cross-country skiing, safaris, surfing, windsurfing, ballooning and ocean sailing). MICE tourism involves small to large groups traveling together for particular purposes usually planned in advance. Within it, "incentive tourism" is a type of company or institution's employee reward for targets

Table 1. Evolution Stages of Costa Rica's Tourist Industry Since the Mid-1980s.

Phase	Pioneer	Growth	Evolution
Market segment	Scientific tourism; Strong interest in ecological tourism	Moderated ecologic tourism; General interest in natural tourism experiences; Sun/beach with natural tourism experience	Sun/beach tourism with moderated adventure tourism; Incentive tourism with natural tourism experiences; Intercultural tourism with natural tourism experiences
Required facilities	Cabins and hostels without any star rating, with 20 rooms or less (basic amenities); Local operators and international operator managing research stations (eco-lodge)	Cabins and hostels ranging from 1 to 3 stars with 20/40 rooms and local operators; Hotels with 3 to 4 stars with 50/80 rooms and local operators; Hotels and hostels with 5 stars increase the market through local operators and foreigners	3 to 5 stars hotels with 50/100 rooms; Local and international operators
Air service and entrance gate	1 Entrance gate (San Jose for regional airlines)	1 Entrance gate (San Jose through regional and international airlines); 1.5 Entrance gates (Liberia for Charter flights)	2 Entrance gates (San Jose/Liberia for both regional and international airlines)
Destination market perception	Strong ecological tourism	Moderate natural tourism	Multifaceted tourism with a difference of strong interest in natural tourism

Source: JICA and ICT (2001, Appendix 1–8).

met or exceeded and unlike other MICEs, it is usually conducted purely for entertainment rather than professional or educational purposes.

Intercultural tourism focuses on gathering new information and experiences to satisfy the tourist's cultural needs. Intercultural tourism relates to a country or region's culture, specifically the lifestyle of the people in the geographical areas, history, art, architecture, religion and other elements that shaped their life style. It includes both urban areas, particularly historic or large cities and their cultural facilities (museums/theatres) and rural areas with the traditions of indigenous cultural communities (i.e., festivals, rituals), and their values and lifestyle.

Industry clusters, are related businesses concentrated in a geographic region, that both locally and globally increase businesses' productivities. Historically, a tourism cluster supports Costa Rica's tourist industry; this cluster comprises many players, mainly lodging, food and transport services, additionally to governmental agencies and related organizations, such as travel agencies. This cluster started to develop during the 1980s, supported by several institutionalized governmental bodies, such as Costa Rica's Ministry of Tourism, founded in 1991, and the Costa Rican Tourism Board, created since 1955, which concentrated and focused all national players' efforts. In addition, other organizations such the National Tourism Chamber, founded in 1974, had historically organized seminars/congresses/workshops, targeting to set a common goal to cluster's players: hotels, travel agencies, transport companies, so that, tourism industry outcomes could be sustainably leveraged on their synergies.

COSTA RICA'S TOURIST INDUSTRY STATUS QUO

Economic Relevance

The tourism industry is of high economic relevance for Costa Rica. It forms part of the country's third tier (service-based sector), which by 2011 represented around 70% of Costa Rica's Gross Domestic Product (GDP). In comparison, the primary tier (agricultural sector) and secondary tier (manufacturing sector) represented 6% and 14%, respectively.

Between 2004 and 2008, the tourism sector contributed an average 7.2% of the GDP. In this regards, Costa Rica places second in the Central American and Caribbean region, only slightly outstripped by the Dominican Republic, where tourism represented 7.8% of its GDP in 2011

(Banco Central de la Republica Dominicana, 2013). In 2011, the Dominican Republic received 4.28 million of visitors, which injected 4.36 billion to the country's economy, representing an average expenditure of US$1,000/visitor. In comparison, in the same year, Costa Rica had 2.19 million international tourist arrivals. They represented US$2.15 billion in international tourism receipts – which also meant an average expense of US$1,000 per tourist (Table 2).

Business Model and National Strategy

A traditional focused on demand tourism development model; adjust itself to customers by satisfying expectations and preferences of particular groups and segments. However, this exclusive business model promotes the construction of artificial destinations totally misaligned with the social, cultural and environmental reality of a country or region. Most of the developments in Costa Rica were carried out under this model in the previous decades.

Nonetheless, Costa Rica's current tourism development goal targets to propel an alternative model, focused on the supply side, promoting the inclusion of the country's social, environmental and cultural realities, and so, fitting an inclusive business model focused on the design of genuine tourism products which allow tourists to adapt and integrate real life experiences to their trips. Costa Rica's international campaign motto "Without Artificial Ingredients", is an agglutinated effort of the tourism industry cluster to strengthen the sustainable tourism element.

The traditional exclusive business model is capital intensive (financial wise), so the new inclusive business model seeks a balance between financial, natural, human and social factors. So that, foreign investment attraction, conservation and rational usage of biodiversity/natural areas, participation/ integration of local communities and preservation of traditions acquire a strategic importance, targeting to strengthen the comparative/ competitive advantages of Costa Rica as a tourism destination.

The growth strategy has been conservative with a 6.6% Compound Average Growth Rate target for the period 2002–2012 (Instituto Costarricense de Turismo, 2007), and aims the consolidation of supply and demand linked-tourist destinations, and so, the Costa Rican Tourism Board has focused on strengthening the three main market segments (ecotourism, sun/beach tourism, and adventure tourism) and on developing new tourist niches, by exploiting four fundamental elements: nature related

Table 2. Tourism Incomes and Exports of Products (2004–2011).

Item	2004	2005	2006	2007	2008	2009	2010	2011
Tourist arrivals to Costa Rica	1,452,926.0	1,679,051.0	1,725,261.0	1,979,789.0	2,089,174.0	1,922,579.0	2,099,829.0	2,192,059.0
Traditional exports (millions of $US)	801.1	769.4	915.1	1,001.7	1,066.9	921.7	1,081.1	1,242.7
Coffee (millions of $US)	197.6	232.7	225.8	251.9	305.0	232.2	257.5	374.9
Banana (millions of $US)	543.4	481.2	620.3	673.0	689.7	622.4	702.9	752.4
Piña (millions of $US)	256.2	324.7	432.8	484.9	572.9	599.7	672.0	715.6
Pinneapple (millions of $US)	110.0	103.2	113.8	120.0	125.7	123.7	59.9	66.0
Tourism (millions of $US)	1,358.5	1,570.1	1,620.9	1,927.4	2,174.1	1,805.8	1,857.6	1,985.4
Total exports (millions of $US)	6,301.5	7,026.4	8,207.3	9,352.7	9,503.7	8,783.7	9,448.1	10,408.4
GDP (millions of $US)	18,595.6	19,961.0	22,528.7	26,267.3	29,847.7	29,241.1	36,217.5	41,007.0
Tourism/GDP ratio (%)	7.3	7.9	7.2	7.3	7.3	6.2	5.1	4.8
Tourism/Exports of goods ratio (%)	21.6	22.3	19.7	20.6	22.9	20.6	19.7	19.1

Source: Instituto Costarricense de Turismo (2012, p. 52).
Note: Translated from Spanish. "Piña" is pineapple in Spanish.

activities, ranking from simple observation to participation; local culture and popular expressions contact; comfortableness and convenience; security.

The entry of more international hotel and tourism related chains with higher standardized products and greater comfort level could be considered as a strategy to create a new offer for a new type of demand, although still leveraged on beach and natural attractors. Although segments may be evolving as more tourists value much more comfort aspects that were not necessarily important elements in the past, a radical change in the demand composition is not considered to have occurred, and so, positioning focuses primarily on actions targeted on the following aspects (Instituto Costarricense de Turismo, 2010): stimulate the preference for Costa Rica's tourist services and products in the market chain; encourage destination recognition by the final customer; distinguish Costa Rica's tourist products and services from the ones marketed by the competition, based on sustainability concepts; improve market knowledge to better serve the needs of different segments; land use planning based on the development centers concept as a base unit, in order to improve local destinations' management; development of local capabilities in order to improve tourist space management; business development, primarily with fostering new products which enhance the experience authenticity.

This cohesion/transition of tourist segments encourages the development of new promising tourist activities to satisfy particular more sophisticated niches such as: cultural, educational, rural, community, philanthropic, health, medical, marine, and gastronomic tourism. From the previous niches it is important to differentiate medical tourism from health tourism, also known as wellness or thermal tourism, which is associated with spas, offering treatments for diverse ailments (rheumatologic, stress, dermatological, beauty treatments, among others). Table 3 shows the country's current tourist portfolio according to the Costa Rican Tourism Board (ICT).

Main Market

Costa Rica is visited by citizens from many parts of the world and so it is important to explore the composition of inbound tourists by region to have an idea on the main income contributors. However, visitors from both Canada and North America have historically represented around 45% of

Table 3.   Portfolio of Tourist Products for Costa Rica.

Macro Products	Potential Products
Beach and sun	Potential development in practically all costal units, in especial in North Guanacaste, Mid-Pacific Puntarenas and the South Caribbean.
Conventional tourist trips (leisure touring)	Particularly important in the Central Valley with one day tours in special to near protected areas and volcanoes and to sites with handcraft strengths and other cultural expressions such as Sarchi, Zarcero among others.
Recreational	Particularly important un the Central Valley, North Guanacaste and Central Pacific, since those regions possess an important offer of complementary activities which enrich the tourist experience. Museums, expositions, music, night life, theaters are expressions of this type of complementary product.
Nature observation	Especial potential for the North Caribbean units, Northern flats, Monteverde, Corcovado, Golfito and the Central Valley. The observation of flora and fauna in all its expressions is highlighted.
Adventure in nature	Development opportunity of all regions, although it is particularly important in the Central Valley, Northern flats, Southern Guanacaste and Southern Caribbean. Rafting, canoeing, hiking and scuba diving are highlighted.
Sport	The water sports are highlighted in especial at the coastal regions, with especial emphasis in Southern Guanacaste, Northern Guanacaste, Puntarenas, Mid Pacific and Southern Caribbean. Sport fishing. Surfing, sailing, scuba diving and canoeing are highlighted. The golf development is also important.
Rural tourism	It is important for Corcovado and Golfito regions, Northern flats, Northern Caribbean and the Central Valley. It basically includes the experience concept of participative work with predefined routes.
Senior citizens	It is more related with the conditions and existing facilities. It is important in the Central Valley, Northern Guanacaste, Mid-Pacific, basically due to all the levels of existing development.
Conventions and congresses	The existing conditions make it to be experienced in the Central Valley mainly. However its full potential has not been exploited just yet.
Cruises	Center in Puntarenas, Caribbean (Limon) and Corcovado-Golfito in the Southern Pacific, with distributions centers to Southern Caribbean and the Central Valley mainly. The activity is reconverted in a one day tour.
Health tourism	Particularly important in the Central Valley and the Northern flats with medical attention traditional products, health care houses, recovering houses, hot springs and others.
Tourism of incentives	Adaptable to the whole country depending on the expectations.

Source: Instituto Costarricense de Turismo (2007, p. 77).
Note: Translated from Spanish.

all international inbounds. For instance in 2011, visitors for the United States represent 40% of the inbound market while Canadian amounted for 6%; with the figures from previous years actually being 45% in 2007, 44% in 2008, 45% in 2009, and 45% in 2010.

As seen on Table 4, the breakdown reveals both opportunities but also threats, as the industry has an evident high direct dependency on the US/Canadian markets.

The Instituto Costarricense de Turismo (2007) defines "best prospects" to be "tourists who had traveled to Costa Rica from their homeland for pleasures purposes, for at least five nights during the past three years and stated to be extremely interested or very interested in visiting the country again." Besides, they plan to travel to either other Central American destinations or South America for pleasure purposes. The "best prospects" studies performed by Tourism National Board actually are intended to specifically identify the potential the US and Canadian markets represent in tourism terms. The fact is that those best prospects have remained unchanged in the previous two studies (Instituto Costarricense de Turismo, 2007, 2010): mainly young adults and adults with high education levels (67% have a college degree) where 58% have household incomes higher than $75K which are characteristics of middle/high class.

Out of the entire best prospects' population, 61.3% of them are between 35 and 64 years old with an average age of 49 years. Most of them organized trips by themselves, and only 17.4% prefer trips in groups.

Country Image and Positioning

Since 2002, Costa Rica has maintained a competitive strategy of destination differentiation, buttressed on natural resources as already stated, as an element for product consumer's perception creation, and thus establishing clear differences with respect to other regional and global destinations. The Instituto Costarricense de Turismo – Costa Rican Tourism Board – (2007, p. 60) points out several main attributes that characterize Costa Rica's branding.

These attributes include the following dimensions. Social and cultural development and its characteristics: Very well defined and rooted values in the Costa Rican society, related to historic abolition of the army in the late 1940s, quality of life, solidarity, and democracy. Three attributes are highlighted: friendship; environmental commitment; professionalization of the arts.

Table 4. Inbound Tourist for North America.

Country/Zone	Years				Variation							
	2007	2008	2009	2010	2011	2007–2008		2008–2009		2009–2010		2010–2011	
						Change	%	Change	%	Change	%	Change	%
Total	1,979,789	2,089,174	1,922,579	2,099,829	2,192,059	109,385	5.5	−166,595	−8.0	177,250	9.2	92,230	4.4
Northern America	953,812	976,561	920,371	1,005,309	1,044,569	22,749	2.4	−56,190	−5.8	84,939	9.2	39,260	3.9
Canada	102,061	109,854	102,471	119,654	133,033	7,793	7.6	−7,383	−6.7	17,183	16.8	13,379	11.2
USA	790,315	807,162	770,129	830,993	858,829	16,847	2.1	−37,033	−4.6	60,864	7.9	27,836	3.3
Mexico	61,436	59,545	47,771	54,662	52,707	−1,891	−3.1	−11,774	−19.8	6,891	14.4	−1,955	−3.6

Source: Instituto Costarricense de Turismo (2012, p. 9).
Note: Translated from Spanish.

Natural richness: Costa Rica holds 5% of world's biodiversity due to the complexity and richness of its ecosystems, under several hierarchy formats: National Parks, Protected Areas and Private Reserves provide accessible tourism attractions. An ample environmental variety offering comprises 12 life zones, ranging from very humid forests to dry forests, all of them related to its geographic position and closeness to oceans. Costa Rica has had an early commitment to nature conservation since the 1970s, by the creation of National Parks Systems throughout the country, which currently have had a recreational and research purpose. The fact that Costa Rica has been a frontrunner in environmental policies related to Payment of Environmental Services (PES) and Clean Developing Mechanisms (CDM) under the Kyoto Protocol framework (Murillo, Kilian, & Castro, 2011), has also supported the country positioning in the international scenario.

The mix of the previous attributes is currently paramount in promoting Costa Rica's tourism bundled products development, simply by catering unsatisfied tourists needs with natural and cultural experiences. The Costa Rican Tourism Board actually advocates for a "unified country image," so all tourist products can revolve and be promoted around it:

> "Mother nature," in addition to the "idiosyncratic characteristics of Costa Rica's citizens," is a common denominator for tourist to practice a number of activities with comfort and security, in different places of the country in relatively short periods of time. (Instituto Costarricense de Turismo, 2007, p. 90)

Even when the increasing criminality is tangible, which creates a negative word of mouth and so tourist's recentness is recognized; the Costa Rican Tourism Board (Instituto Costarricense de Turismo, 2007, p. 72), encourages country image to be supported and managed nationwide, based on common tourist products' attributes and on a number of identified comparative advantages: national parks and accessible biodiversity through the current road and highway network, because despite the fact they are generally in an unsuitable shape, they still provide access to many destination points; Costa Rica's effective environmental protection policies; small size country, allowing switching between microclimates in short periods of time; the idiosyncrasy of the average Costa Rican citizen, characterized by his/her kindness; closeness to its main market: USA; a relative better public service infrastructure for catering the tourism markets in comparison to its surrounding neighbors; wide and consolidated development of specialized tourism companies, working in a cluster fashion, with a high degree of experience in Costa Rican tourism products' management.

For instance, the perception of the US tourist about Costa Rica is very positive − 80% consider the country has one of the richest varieties of flora and fauna in the world, 78% are considering to visit the country again, 75% consider is a quiet and peaceful place, 72% consider is a place where they can picture themselves, 71% feel the US citizen is welcomed (Instituto Costarricense de Turismo, 2010). Besides its exotic nature, without a doubt, the closeness of Costa Rica to the United States and Canada is paramount in their decision to visit Costa Rica.

THE MEDICAL INDUSTRY AND MEDICAL TOURISM WORLDWIDE

Medical Industry Worldwide

The global medical industry is one of the world's fastest growing industries, absorbing over 10% of GDP of most developed nations, amounting a total health care expenditure of $4.5 trillion in 2012 (The Medica, 2013). The industry comprises an ample range of services: hospitals, physicians, nursing homes, diagnostic laboratories, pharmacies, drugs, pharmaceuticals, chemicals, medical equipment, manufacturers, and suppliers. Factors such as increasing government involvement, the aging population combine to technological advancements poses challenges to the industry.

The United States, along with Switzerland and Germany, represent the largest medical and health care industries in the world, where the United States has the largest workforce as 1 out of every 11 US residents is employed in the health care industry and with approximately 3.8 million daily inpatient visits and 20 million outpatients ones (*ibid.*, 2013). According to Plunkett Research (2013) the total US health care expenditures were estimated to be $2.8 trillion in 2012, representing about 17.9% of GDP, and are projected to soar to $3.5 trillion in 2016.

Global Overview of Medical Tourism

According to Connell (2006, p. 2), medical tourism, also known as medical travel, health travel, global health care, medical treatment abroad, is a practice "where people travel often-long distances to overseas destinations to obtain medical, dental and surgical care while simultaneously being holi-daymakers, in a more conventional sense."

Places like Baden-Baden in Germany, Bath in the United Kingdom and Karlovy Vary in the Czech Republic once burgeon as curative health spas because of their natural thermal springs. During the 20th century, tradition-ally, patients from developing countries often traveled to more developed ones in order to attend medical centers, where they received the health ser-vices that were not available in their home countries.

During the 21st century, as medical know-how and technology became available and spread out over less developed nations, the new model of medical tourism actually evolved, as tourists from rich countries are cur-rently exploiting the possibility of combining both medical and tourist aspects. According to a study from McKinsey & Company, medical tour-ism revenues amounted $40 billion worldwide in 2004, $60 billion in 2006 (Herrick, 2008), $79 billion in 2010 and it is expected to increase to 130 bil-lion by 2015, as a study by KPMG (Richter, 2012) describes.

Traditionally, the most common medical tourism treatments were den-tal and cosmetic surgery; however, currently there is a high demand of medical treatments in infertility or orthopedics, such as, hip replacement, hip resurfacing, knee replacements, basically due to the fact that proce-dures usually do not have complications or require significant follow up care or even is hiking up to more complex interventions such as cardiac surgeries. This practice is rapidly growing as patients receive either equal or even greater care than they would have received in their home coun-tries. To minimize the risk of traveling soon after surgery or simply to take full advantage of the trip, medical tourist patients often combine their medical trips with vacation time set aside for resting and recovery in the destination country.

The fact is that medical tourism is greater move toward a globalization phenomenon in health care which comprises: (a) re-importation of drugs from abroad, (b) "brain drain" or importation of health care providers, (c) research tourism, where pharmaceutical companies based in particular country perform clinical trials abroad, and (d) telemedicine, where services are provided remotely and so both patients and providers remain in their respective countries.

Although the proportion is tending to change, a majority of the interna-tional patients are self-insured and they have become more medically savvy, supported by the worldwide explosion in access to information about health care. Some other patients have not insurance whatsoever, so they cover the treatment costs totally out of their pockets (Cook, 2009).

According to Alessie (2009) four key factors are explanatory of the industry growth worldwide.

(1) Quality and price: An increasing number of hospitals are gaining international accreditation. In addition, "local hospitals" are going global, as for instance in recent years leading US hospitals such as the Mayo Clinic and Johns Hopkins have set up offshore operations in the Middle East and Asia. Common surgical procedures can be performed in these hospitals for about a fifth or less of the price charged in their home country hospitals.

(2) Convenience and speed: In countries where public health care systems operate could take considerable time to get non-urgent medical care. For example, in the United Kingdom and Canada it could take one year to get a hip replacement, while in Thailand, this could be done within a week.

(3) Global economy: Many people no longer live exclusively in their countries of origin and are becoming increasingly mobile in both their temporary and permanent work assignments. Global citizens are willing to pay for health care which matches their global lifestyle.

(4) Global private health insurance coverage: The emergence of "global citizens" have pushed several private health insurance companies to launch global "coverage products" which include costs of transportation, as a requisite to stay competitive.

Given the attractive growth forecasts of this sector, various countries are trying to promote themselves as "health care destinations". The high potential of the industry is giving incentives in many world regions to enter the business. As an example, the Middle East has tried to learn from the top medical tourism destinations in order to create "local brands" to attract international patients and insurance companies. In particular, the Dubai Healthcare City project has been designed not only to attract medical tourists but also to reduce the need for residents to travel abroad to receive high quality treatment.

Mass medical tourism is expected to be originated in developed countries (United States or Europe), due to their relatively high purchasing power in comparison to developing countries' purchasing power. However, the major inflow of global tourists is to be expected from the United States, due to a simple reason: European countries count on state-funded systems which amid the existence of waiting lists still provide patients the chance to get medical treatment in their home countries for whether free or reasonable costs.

Nevertheless, European patients, as they start getting fed up of those long waiting lists and start realizing of the relative low costs of paying for treatments abroad and the easiness of reaching the services, might start grossing up the global inflow figures of medical tourism worldwide. It is to mention that the relative closeness of the country of treatment to the country of origin plays a paramount role in the decision. However, the future development of the worldwide market is still unclear and several international research companies keep a close eye on the sector due to its potential to become increasingly global.

Potential of the US Market

After WWII the health care industry experienced a tremendous growth in the United States with paying a close attention to efficiency, productivity and competition; with employers, federal and state governments covering such big proportion of the health care bill, that patients became not sensitive to medical attention costs.

The US federal government's health care program for 65 years or older citizens, known as Medicare, covered 50.7 million seniors in 2012, where nationwide expenditures were projected to be $590.8 billion, including premiums paid by beneficiaries. Due to the massive number of "baby boomers" entering retirement age, by 2030 the current figure will gross up to about 78.0 million (Plunkett Research, 2013). Complementary, the federal government's health care program for low-income, disabled persons (including children), and certain groups of seniors in nursing homes, known as Medicaid, sum up national expenditures of $458.9 billion in 2012. Although heavily supported by the federal government, the different states also contribute significantly, which represent a significant burden to their budgets (Plunkett Research, 2013).

The rising costs of health care in the United States, growing at rate of 6.5% since 2000 (Rosenthal, 2009) which surpasses the inflation rate; is hitting medical services consumers and payers and so causing a tremendous problem when facing surgical procedures. In addition employers are also hammered by increases in costs for health coverage provision to employees and retirees. For instance, in accordance to Plunkett Research (2013) when citing a report from the Kaiser Family Foundation it was estimated that in 2012 an employer's premium cost to cover an average family amounted $15,745 per year (a 102% increase since 2002) with the average worker paying 27% ($4,316) of that premium.

The main actors of the health care scenario are all experiencing some problems and looking for new alternatives. Many major employers are putting into place unique new programs to reduce employees' illnesses their related costs; to the extent that in the case of very large employers in-house physicians and nurses are being hired as a way to provide workplace primary and preventive care. Patients and insurance companies are facing the increase in prescription drug costs and new medical technologies. Patients by themselves are putting pressure on insurance companies as they are demanding high plan flexibility when choosing MDs and specialists at their will. Hospitals and health systems are wiping out high amounts of revenues to bad debt, and so increasing costs for non-arrear patients.

Although in March 2010, President Obama signed the Patient Protection and Affordable Care Act, designed to strengthen insurance company regulation and provide medical coverage to more than 30 million uninsured Americans, and amid the huge investment in health care made, 16% of citizens, amounting 48.6 million, lacked health care coverage for the entire year of 2011 (Plunkett Research, 2013); since for some of them insurances were either unavailable or unaffordable or simply responded to the personal decision of not to pay for it. A great amount of uninsured are illegal immigrants, and as stated by Plunkett Research (2013) when citing a Kaiser Family Foundation study named *Medicaid and the Uninsured* dated from February 2007, it was reported that one-fourth of the uninsured were eligible for public programs but were not enrolled: mainly low-income children and in some cases their parents. In addition, up to date and in accordance to the National Institute of Dental and Craniofacial Research (2013) around 108 million US citizens (both children and adults) lack dental health plans. Those numbers are expected to grow along with health care costs.

The previous figures, of uninsured and sub insured citizens might represent a huge market for medical tourism services. In addition, and even when only about 11% of employers in the United States offer benefit options abroad in accordance to a survey conducted by the International Foundation of Employee Benefit Plans as cited in Herrick (2008), insured citizens who are not willing to pay high deductibles or have low reimbursement rates also represent a fertile market for medical tourism.

Currently, the typical US medical tourist appears to have been uninsured or underinsured, chasing for substantial cost savings in health care. A potential medical tourist could be described as someone not poor enough to be eligible for government assistance but not wealthy enough to pay out of his own pocket a ranging $50k to $80k hip replacement in a US hospital. The fact and the matter is that more recently, state governments, self-insured firms, Fortune 500 companies, and domestic insurers are putting pressure on their insurers to use medical tourism either as a requirement or through the provision of incentives (Cohen, 2010).

According to Piazolo and Zanca (2011) in 2005 approximately 500,000 US citizens traveled abroad for medical treatment; figure that rose to 750,000 by 2007 and it is expected to increase to more than 15 million per year by 2017, based on the US market outbound projection model (see Fig. 1) from Deloitte (2008).

In 2007, the ¾ of a million US outbound patients represented a total expense of $2.1 billion in health care abroad. According to Deloitte (2008)

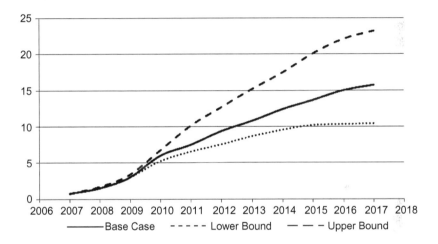

		2007	2008	2009	2010	2011	2012	2013	2014	2015	2016	2017
Base Case	Patients (millions)	0.75	1.5	3	6	7.5	9.38	10.78	12.39	13.64	15	15.75
	Growth (Rate %)	100	100	100	25	25	15	15	10	10	5	
Lower Bound	Patients (millions)	0.75	1.5	3	5.25	6.56	7.55	8.68	9.55	10.2	10.32	10.43
	Growth (Rate %)	100	100	75	25	15	15	10	5	3	1	
Upper Bound	Patients (millions)	0.75	1.69	3.38	6.75	10.13	12.66	15.19	17.47	20.09	22.09	23.2
	Growth (Rate %)	125	100	100	50	20	20	15	10	10	10	

Fig. 1. USA Outbound Patient Flow, 10-Year Projection (Millions). *Assumptions*: In 2007, approximately 750,000 Americans traveled outbound for medical care. That number will increase to six million by 2010. Therefore, the growth rate from 2007 to 2010 is 100% for the base case estimate; after 2010, the growth rate will begin to fall due to supply capacity constraints in foreign countries; upper/lower bound estimates assume the growth rate is higher/lower than the base case estimate, as shown in table. *Source*: The author with data from Deloitte (2008, pp. 3–4).

and its model, the outbound medical tourist market of US patients will have a potential of between $30.3 to $79.5 billion by 2017 (see Fig. 2), resulting in a potential opportunity cost of $228.5−599.5 billion to US health care providers.

Although, the 2008 financial crisis was a factor that forced US citizens to look for less expensive medical treatments abroad, it also caused a purchasing power reduction which impacted the industry as patients did not have enough economic resources to face expenditures for non-lifethreatening surgeries like cosmetic surgery, dentistry, and laser procedures.

US patients and potential medical travelers are basically looking into Latin-American medical infrastructure, because of a proximity factor, where in some cases even better treatments is provided when compared to the US health care system: VIP services, attentive nurses, frequent email communication with MDs seem to be key decision factors for the patients. According a report from Deloitte (2009) Costa Rica, Brazil, Mexico were the only three Latin American countries which had been identified by US

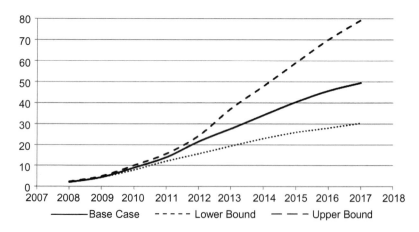

		2008	2009	2010	2011	2012	2013	2014	2015	2016	2017
Base Case	Spending (billions U.S.$)	2.1	4.4	9	13.9	21.4	27.6	34.1	40.4	45.7	49.5
Lower Bound	Spending (billions U.S.$)	2.1	4.4	7.9	12.1	15.6	19.3	22.9	25.9	28	30.3
Upper Bound	Spending (billions U.S.$)	2.4	4.9	10.1	15.6	24.1	37.2	47.9	59.2	70.2	79.5

Fig. 2. American Medical Association Guidelines for Patients Traveling Overseas for Medical Care. *Note*: The weighted price of a procedure in a foreign country as multiplied by the flow of outbound US patients. Inflation-adjusted using a rate of 3%. *Source*: The author with data from Deloitte (2008, p. 14).

patients in 2008 for possessing at least one accredited hospital capable of providing medical tourism services.

Choosing the right medical facility abroad, a one complying with safe and high quality care standards regarding infrastructure and staff, has become primary concern, as the number of hospitals, clinics and spas offering medical tourism services has burgeoned.

Several factors are paramount when doing the election. These factors include the following steps: a certification from the most recognizable accreditation bodies; count with MDs and care teams trained under western standards; count with reputable, top level US medical providers, facilities and/or teaching hospitals affiliations; technology matching the one in western hospitals, both medical equipment wise and clinical information.

As expected, the previous requirements pose challenges to potential patients which coupled to the potential market of medical tourism explains the emergence of several new players. Medical travel intermediaries or medical tourism facilitators work as specialized travel agents offering services for coordinating and accompanying potential patients during their whole treatment experience. The main service these firms provide are to find doctors and hospitals, help patients with visa requirements, find best deals on airfare and hotel rooms, find ground transportation, translators and local liaisons to guide the patient and serve as his/her advocate in case of problems.

The fact those companies investigate medical providers abroad to ensure quality and screen patients to assess those who are physically suitable to travel, often by having a staff of MDs/nurses evaluating the medical efficacy of the procedures to be provided, and so aiding patients in selecting medical facilities and MDs. If the role is those companies is extended, they actually become accreditation bodies which assess the quality of hospital services and so become an important reputation creator agents. For instance the World Med Assist Company has strategic relationships with hospitals like Johns Hopkins and Harvard Medical and supports patients to find affordable treatment overseas. Other brokerages such us Planet Hospital, Global Med Network, Med Journeys, and Med Retreat also provide similar services.

Besides accreditation purposes, other organizations also play extremely important roles in the medical tourism industry. The following mentioned comprise the most important organizations within the industry. ISQua (The International Society for Quality in Healthcare) is a non-profit, independent organization with members in over 100 countries, providing services to guide health professionals, providers, researchers, agencies, policy makers and consumers, to achieve excellence in health care delivery to all people, and to continuously improve the quality and safety of care. Joint Commission International targets to improve the safety of patient care through the provision of accreditation and certification services as well as through advisory and educational services, which target is to help organizations in the implementation of practical and sustainable solutions.

A key element for the medical tourism providers (hospitals, ambulatory care facilities, clinical laboratories, care continuum services, medical transport organizations, and primary care services) is the Joint Commission International (JCI) Accreditation, which is a "quality seal of approval", certifying hospitals, laboratories, medical transport organizations, care continuum (non-acute settings from assisted living to private homes), ambulatory care, and primary care providers meet high performance standards and giving health care organizations access to a variety of resources and services that connect them with the international community. Additionally, organizations can also pursue Clinical Care Program Certification to demonstrate excellence in the integration and coordination of care for specific diseases. JCI has certified organizations in 90 countries.

Medical Tourism Association or Medical Travel Association is non-profit international organization which helps patients to identify hospitals and organizations accredited by the Joint Commission International. Patients can locate information about MDs, their area of expertise and rate of success on the medical procedures they perform on the organizations' website. It is actually an international branch of the Joint Commission Resources, working since 1994 with health care organizations, health departments in several countries and global organizations. Accredited by ISQua since 2007, assures that approved JCI standards, training and processes meet the highest international benchmarks for accreditation bodies.

American Association for Accreditation of Ambulatory Surgery Facilities (AAAASF) which develops and implements standards to ensure patient care quality through an accreditation program both serves the medical community and the general public, establishing means for measuring medical competence and providing an external source for patients' safety assessment in the ambulatory surgery setting. It certifies both surgery facilities and insurance carriers.

Accreditation Association for Ambulatory Health Care (AAAHC): a private, non-profit organization that since 1979 develops standards to promote patient safety, quality and value for ambulatory health care through peer-based accreditation processes, education and research.

Other important players are the still skeptical and risk-adverse insurance companies. According to the "global patient" point of view, if it is cheaper for the uninsured patient to go global, it is cheaper also for the insurer. The main goal in this emerging industry is patients, employers, insurance companies end up paying less. The potential lawsuits associated to malpractices have made some of the largest US insurance providers unwilling to cover procedures performed abroad. Currently insurers are slowly testing the medical services outside the United States. In this sense, US outbound medical tourism is still in its infancy since insurers are not massively taking advantage of the medical incentives abroad.

Medical tourism advocates hope to encourage greater competition among global health care providers, leading to lower prices and better care within the United States where some hospitals have taken notice of their global competitors and are working to cut prices.

Several factors pose concerns about the industry, and someone may represent growth limits to the industry. These factors include the following dimensions:

(1) Ability to secure follow-up care once patients return to the United States; some U.S. MDs may not be willing to handle long-term patients for procedures they were not involved in.
(2) Patients' recourse in the event of malpractice; if anything goes wrong during a procedure in a foreign country, the patient has to work through the host country's legal system, which represents a difficulty for the customer.
(3) US legal health care policies: Besides the recent 2012 health reform, another future substantial one, to make the health system more affordable would completely kill the market for medical tourism.

Although several organizations now have protocols to aid patients seeking medical care abroad, the whole medical tourism industry has remained unstructured in general terms, lacking relevant legislation to rule the main players' practices, and so remaining a subject of great debate.

In order to provide some sort of direction within the industry as it continues to grow, the American Medical Association (AMA) issued a nine guidelines (Deloitte, 2009, p. 4) set to be followed by employers, insurance companies and other bodies that facilitate or incentivize medical care abroad. (1) Medical care outside the United States should be voluntary. (2) Financial incentives to go outside the United States for care should not inappropriately limit diagnostic and therapeutic alternatives, or restrict treatment or referral options. (3) Financial incentives should be used only for care at institutions certified by international recognized accrediting bodies. (4) Local follow-up care should be coordinated and financing arranged to ensure continuity of care. (5) Coverage for travel outside the United States for care must include the costs of follow-up care upon return. (6) Patients should be informed of rights and legal recourse before traveling outside the United States for care. (7) Patients should have access to physician licensing and outcomes data, as well as facility accreditation and outcomes data. (8) Transfer of patient medical records should be consistent with The Health Insurance Portability and Accountability Act (HIPAA) guidelines, which protects health insurance coverage for workers and their families when they change or lose their jobs. (9) Patients should be provided with information about the potential risks of combining surgical procedures with long flights and vacation activities.

MEDICAL TOURISM IN COSTA RICA

The Early Stages

In 1971, a new retiring bill was approved in Costa Rica, which entitled about 40,000 retired foreigners establish for living. As expected they required of health care services which created a niche for local MDs, which in turn started to provide services to their patients' relatives who started to arrive into the country as the word of mouth of "less expensive treatments" spread out. Those treatments were especially cosmetic or dental and were provided for a fraction of the price of what it would have been paid in the United States under the same or higher quality standards.

Pioneer doctors, where MD. Pino was the first mover (Cook, 2009), and clinics used to put efforts individually, promoting their services in isolated campaigns and basically levering communication by the word of mouth and later on through the use of webpages. The logistics required, were actually coordinated by the MDs themselves in many cases.

In order to take advantage of the growing plastic surgery/dental treatments and yearly medical check-ups trends, the private hospitals in the country such as the Clinica Biblica Hospital and Clinica Catolica started individual efforts to attract tourists during the 1990s. Later on, the CIMA Hospital, appeared in the private health scenario in Costa Rica.

The Clinica Bíblica Hospital, founded in 1929, is the largest private hospital in Costa Rica with a JCI accreditation, comprising a wide variety of medical treatments ranging from lifethreatening emergencies to leading-edge procedures, medical checkups or facelifts. The Clínica

Católica, is another private hospital also JCI accredited, founded in 1963 by a group of nuns and MDs as an alternative offer to Costa Rica's public health system. The JCI accredited CIMA Hospital is one of the four hospitals of the Hospital International, S.A de C.V (CHI) Consortia, which is the Mexican affiliate of International Hospital Corporation (headquartered in Dallas, Texas) and which invests, operates and markets specialized hospitals, under the brand CIMA (Centro International de Medicina).

After 2005, most of the MDs and clinics involved in the medical tourism business, basically offered services on plastic surgery and cosmetic surgery (15% together), cosmetic dentistry and dental treatments (35% together) and bariatric surgery and medical check-ups (50% together), targeting both national and international patients, offering interactive web pages and connections abroad in order reach the offshore market. Some of those clinics went ahead and sought certifications of international credited agencies, such as American Association for Accreditation of Ambulatory Surgery Facilities (AAAASF) and the Accreditation Association for Ambulatory Health Care (AAAHC).

Industry Market Estimates

According to Euromonitor (2013) the market size of medical tourism in Costa Rica represented $159 million in 2011, figure that placed the country in the 46% percentile of the worldwide countries offering medical tourism services. The local medical industry is actually expected to grow until 2016 at a 6.2% compound average growth rate, which places the country on a 64% percentile position out of the rest of the countries in the study (Euromonitor, 2013). Although Herrick (2007) reported that in 2006, 150,000 foreigners sought medical care in Costa Rica, this figure is thought to be quite overestimated since as reported by Manzi (2009) in 2007 around 30,000 medical tourists arrived to Costa Rica, figure that rose up to 40,000 by 2010 (Central America Data, 2013b).

Up to date, and in accordance to Central America Data (2013a), as reported by the Costa Rica Tourism Board, in 2012 there were 48,000 inbound patients to Costa Rica, most of them from United States and Canada with an average expenditure of $7,000, which represented a total revenue of $338 million for the country. The 2012 figures increased by 4%, as the total revenue of $300 million was reached in 2011, figure that totally surpassed Euromonitor's above mentioned market size. The previous figures are expected to reach 100,000 medical tourists, representing total revenue of $800 million by 2014 (Central America Data, 2013a).

Many Costa Rican MDs have done their studies abroad, either in the United States or Europe. Most of the plastic surgeons had obtained their specialization abroad in special in the United States and so, most of them and their staff speaks English fluently.

Up the date, the greatest demand for medical tourism services comprises odontology (42%), orthopedics y gynecology (22%), preventive medicine (16%), and plastic surgery (10%) (Central America Data, 2013a). See Table 5, for comparative prices of the United States to Colombia and Costa Rica, based on 2011 prices.

Table 5. Price Comparison for Different Medical Treatment in Different Countries (2011 Prices).

Medical Procedure	USA	Colombia	Costa Rica
Heart Bypass	$144,000	$14,802	$25,000
Angioplasty	$57,000	$4,500	$13,000
Heart Valve Replacement	$170,000	$18,000	$30,000
Hip Replacement	$50,000	$6,500	$12,500
Hip Resurfacing	$50,000	$10,500	$12,500
Knee Replacement	$50,000	$6,500	$11,500
Spinal Fusion	$100,000	N/A	$11,500
Dental Implant	$2,800	$1,750	$900
Lap Band	$30,000	$9,900	$8,500
Breast Implants	$10,000	$2,500	$3,800
Rhinoplasty	$8,000	$2,500	$4,500
Face Lift	$15,000	$5,000	$6,000
Hysterectomy	$15,000	N/A	$5,700
Gastric Sleeve	$28,700	$7,200	$10,500
Gastric Bypass	$32,972	$9,900	$12,500
Liposuction	$9,000	$2,500	$3,900
Tummy Tuck	$9,750	$3,500	$5,300
Lasik (both eyes)	$4,400	$2,000	$1,800
Cornea (both eyes)	N/A	N/A	$4,200
Retina	N/A	N/A	$4,500
IVF Treatment	N/A	N/A	$2,800

Source: Medical Tourism (2013).

Note: Prices are approximate and not actual prices and include estimated airfare for patient and companion. Prices will vary based upon many factors including hospital, doctor's experience, accreditation, currency exchange rates and more. Costs for meals, miscellaneous expenses and any hotel costs or tourism costs are excluded.

Cluster Evolution

According to Manzi (2009), medical tourism had been until recently only recognized as a complementary service to the main tourism niches, as only rural, community and MICE tourism had stood out and had been identified by Costa Rican Tourism Board, which role had been more reactive than proactive during the last decade, as the most promising future development tourism alternatives. The Costa Rican government recognized that in order to reach the critical mass for medical tourism to take off, an unconditional commitment and joint efforts were required, not only from the main direct players (private hospital, clinics, recovery centers, independent MDs, local insurance companies, local travel agencies), but also from local universities, and related governmental agencies. Thus, in November 2006, the Costa Rican government showed its high commitment to medical tourism when the topic was included in the Costa Rican Competitiveness National Department's Competitiveness Agenda, targeting to increase health services and the additional development of related services, and so, setting the foundations to create a medical tourism cluster (Manzi, 2009).

The vision of the Competitiveness National Department was to induce the same clustering effect that Costa Rica experienced when the Intel microcircuits company started operations in the mid-1990s. It was stated the real need to promote a consolidated biotechnology, pharmaceuticals and medical research industry, in order to position Costa Rica as a world class destination for medical tourism and as a center for complex high quality medicine.

Besides the Competitiveness National Department, there were additional bodies highly committed to create a medical tourism cluster: the Costa Rican Health National Department; the Procomer agency, which is a non-governmental public agency officially responsible for promoting Costa Rican exports; the International Trade National Department and naturally the Costa Rican Tourism Board and the Tourism National Department. The role of the Health National Department was paramount in this industry, since public health is a vital condition for the industry development (*ibid.*, 2009).

The medical tourism industry, offers the Health National Department, the potential benefit to create a source of revenue, by renting idle operating rooms during the night, since for a few specific treatments public hospital's equipment infrastructure surpasses the private one's (low demand in some specialties does not justify the investment in some equipment) (*ibid.*, 2009). One the main issues to be solved is the "health quality seals" for all the players (*ibid.*, 2009).

The potential of the medical tourism is substantial, and implies incentives for more new players to appear, which have organizing themselves and aggregating to become an industry cluster. In February 2009, the Costa Rican government declared medical tourism industry a "national interest matter", by issuing a national bill. In order to agglutinated all the isolated players' efforts and aligned them toward a common effort, the government propelled the formation of Promed (Council for International Promotion of Costa Rica Medicine), as the official agency to promote and regulate the medical tourism industry nationwide, as a mean to widen the current international services' portfolio, as well as channel to attract direct foreign investment and to multiply the clustering effects associated. Promed promotes a joint sustainable effort of the public and private sectors, without regulating or deciding on any government tourism-related policies. The idea is to provide competitiveness benefits to all sectors, agencies and companies involved in the medical tourism value chain, such as medicine, tourism, science, technology, and pharmaceutical and medical equipment industries. Promed's target has been to concentrate on non-complex surgeries, creating excellent services in general medicine.

However, according to Manzi (2009) its future strategy is to develop offerings in more complex surgeries, for which medical specializations are required, and so, hospitals have been identified as key players. Although no concrete investments had been made to the moment, several internationally well-known US hospitals had shown their interest in starting operations in Costa Rica, such as the Mayo Clinic, Cleveland Hospital, Baptist Hospital, Harvard Hospital, Jackson Memorial Hospital and the famous John Hopkins which actually operates in Panama in a franchise fashion (Manzi, 2009).

Locally, shortage of nurses, technician staff (X-ray operators for instance) and specialist MDs have been identified as restrictive factors in the medical tourism development, in particular because a the great number of MDs are only devoted only to work for the national health system agency (CCSS) as there is a lack of incentives to fully enter in the medical tourism industry. Besides, CENDEISS (Strategic and Information Development Center for Health and Social Security) is a dependency from the national health system agency (CCSS), in charge of training medical staff, has a policy which is perceived as inefficient regarding the future supply of technicians and, particularly, specialists: only medical students from the University of Costa Rica, which is the biggest public university considered to provide the best high education in the country and the only state-funded institution providing MDs for the national system, have access to specialization in public hospitals. This policy has to be more flexible and allow students from private universities to do so too. In order to leverage the provision of qualified human resource for future expansion, an alliance between the private hospitals involved to the medical tourism industry (CIMA/Clinica Biblica/Clinica Catolica Hospital) and CENDEISS, seems like a viable solution.

The international insurances companies in the United States are also paramount players in local development, because they drive demand of the most suitable service providers. A trustful method must be developed in order to get reimbursements through the Medicare system in the United States. Players' joint local efforts may escalate to win-win negotiations with the international insurance carriers within two or three years. It has been estimated that partnerships with 10 or 30 insurance companies would be enough for Costa Rica to reach the large business volume required to leverage the medical-tourism cluster creation (*ibid.*, 2009). Most US patients rely on health plans to determine treatment options available, and thus several US insurers have initiated medical tourism pilot programs within their health benefits (see Table 6), with expectations to reduce costs and improve margins, while employers are seeking health care costs reductions.

Whether these pilots will be adopted on a broad scale and whether employers or patients will receive costs' savings benefits via reduced premiums, co-payments or deductibles is yet to be determined (Deloitte, 2009). Unfortunately, to the best of the author's knowledge, none of those pilot programs have been started in Costa Rica or the region just yet.

One of ProMed's main efforts is to promote international missions to US tourist conventions, basically targeting to reach insurance providers. Marketing is not focused on end users or potential patients in this case, as done in traditional magazines ads, but intends to reach massive publics, by posting on the New York Times and the Travel and Living channels.

According to Duar (2009) ProMed projects focus on developing medical treatments and surgical procedures; deontologist, ophthalmology, plastic and aesthetic surgery, urology, cardiovascular surgery, orthopedics, bariatric, and general surgery; post-surgery care, physiotherapy and rehabilitation; medical checkups.

In addition, the Costa Rican National Standards Agency (INTECO) actually developed a national accreditation of quality seal for organizations related to the medical tourism industry, in the very same way the JCI create its own standards: (1) Tourism for Health, focused on organizations providing lodging services, travel agencies, tour operators specialized in medical tourism and transport companies. (2) Allied-Health Services, companies

Table 6. Medical Tourism Pilot Programs Within Health Benefits Plans.

Insurer	State	Foreign Medical Site	Program Summary
Anthem Blue Cross Anthem Blue Cross and Blue Shield (WellPoint)	Wisconsin	Apollo Hospitals, India	• Will send the employees of Serigraph Inc., a corporate client of Anthem WellPoint, to Apollo Hospitals for certain elective procedures; the program will start with Delhi and Bangalore facilities and later expand to all JCI-accredited Apollo Hospitals • Pilot project will cover about 700 group members • All financial details, including travel and medical arrangements, will be managed by Anthem WellPoint
United Group Program	Florida	Bummigrad, Thailand Apollo Hospitals, India	• Actively promoting medical tourism to more than 200,000 individuals covered through self-funded health plans and fully insured, mini-med plans
Blue Shield and Health Net	California	Mexico	• Covers about 20,000 patients • Focused on employers that hire a large number of Mexican immigrants
Blue Cross Blue Shield	South Carolina	Bummigrad, Thailand	• Will cover patients' procedures organized through Companion Global if their plans cover travel • Will also cover two follow-up visits with physicians at Doctors Care

Source: Deloitte (2009, p. 5).

manufacturing medical and health products, pharmaceuticals, consulting, dental labs, drugstores, clinical labs and companies devoted in developing medical tourism infrastructure. (3) Recovery and Health, medical assistance providing services to patients, recovery centers, spas, yoga centers, elderly retirement homes, holistic medicine centers.

According to Central America Data (2013b) based on information provided by ProMed Costa Rica, up to date there are around 300 companies part of this cluster, including hotels, hospitals, clinics, recovery centers, tourism operators which in turn generate around 20,000 direct and indirect jobs.

The Regional Competition

Cuba has historically had an extremely knowledgeable, skilled and prepared medical staff as far as non-traditional medicine concerns, the fact that they lack of infrastructure and the modern technology required by the medical tourism industry discards the country as a potential competitor in the forthcoming years.

According to Yanos (2008) based on quality and affordability of care as well as receptiveness to foreign investment, the top five medical tourism destinations in 2008 were Panama, Brazil, Costa Rica Malaysia, and India. According to a Pacific Prime (2012) publication the top five medical destination in 2012 were Thailand, India, Costa Rica, Panama, Malaysia. The fact and the matter is that within the region, both Panama and Costa Rica seem to have a high steady place on the medical tourism marketplace, which stresses the potential of the industry for both countries.

Within the region, Colombia and El Salvador have been identified as competitors for Costa Rica. However, even when having the infrastructural resources, Colombia has the negative factor of personal security perception and in El Salvador, even when a few clinics have been identified to offer similar services as the ones in Costa Rica, it also exists a negative perception due to low business volume (Manzi, 2009).

Bearing the latter in mind, Panama could be seen as Costa Rica's main regional direct competitor, since as above mentioned it belongs to "the top five medical travel destination world club." Medical care Panama could be less from 40% all the way to 70% costs in the United States (Herrick, 2007), provided in high quality health care facilities concentrated primarily in the metropolitan areas, where medical standards at top hospitals are comparable to US ones; and many local physicians possess training in the

United States (for instance, the Punta Pacifica Hospital is affiliated to Johns Hopkins International).

However, Panama is not perceived as a threat to Costa Rica as it is considered it lacks of the potential to challenge Costa Rica from a country awareness creation perspective. Despite its economic resources to develop infrastructure, it lacks of a comparable structural human capital and know-how in the tourism matters which are vital features of a fairly good organized industry cluster (Manzi, 2009).

According to ProMed, Brazil and Mexico are Costa Rica's main competitors (Central America Data, 2013b). However, when compared to Mexico (basically concentrated on dental treatment), even when proximity is a positive factor for US patients (travelling by road from next-door states such as California or Texas takes only one day trip) the insecurity perception represents a drawback when attracting medical tourists, in especial when the US State Department is often issuing security warnings. The fact is that the traveling time from the United States to Costa Rica is not as time consuming, depending on the departure state, basically because of the offering of several direct flights, bounded to Costa Rica's current high developed natural tourism industry. In the case of Brazil, distance becomes a drawback for medical tourism patient who may prefer to travel to Costa Rica.

MEDICAL TOURISM BRANDING

Up to date, according to Instituto Costarricense de Turismo (2010), besides recognizing MICE, rural, senior and social tourism as new potential products to complement Costa Rica's traditional offer, medical tourism has also been included as it is conceptually close related to Costa Rica tourist product base and the values it possess, which are associated to the tourist product: authenticity, mental peace, experience, character and sense of belonging, among the most relevant. Without a doubt, developing the medical tourism product requires of infrastructure, especially surgery and recovery specialized centers, besides leisure and health centers. According to the Instituto Costarricense de Turismo (2010) the Costa Rica's medical tourist offering is to offer a mix of surgical, esthetical and dental procedures in a fast and less expensive fashion (compared to patients' countries of origin) and activities designed around the provision of those health services.

ProMed's objective is to transform Costa Rica in one of the main destinations for medical tourism within Latin America (Central America Data, 2013b). According to survey from the Instituto Costarricense de Turismo (2010), when US citizens are interviewed about the possible countries they would travel for surgery, they mention three to four countries. The target is that Costa Rica could be included within those four countries and in the long run cut into the top of mind category, in the same way natural tourism distinguishes Costa Rica internationally in the tourists' minds.

Medical tourism development has to rely on the already exiting natural tourism destination brand. The current potential to create this medical tourism destination brand is extremely high, buttressed by the competitive advantages that already distinguish Costa Rica: geographic position, climate conditions, political, economic stability, and environmental protection commitment.

CONCLUSIONS

Medical tourist growth requires development of new products, in order to either robust the existing complementary segments or develop and commercialize new segments, capable of diversifying and strengthen the market mix. For the emerging rural tourism, MICE tourism, and the potential medical tourism products, the SMEs clustering current focus is required in order to maintain the actual integration momentum of all the players into a competitive value chain.

As a matter of fact, the emergence of the medical tourism cluster, aggregating all of stakeholders under one umbrella is actually a sign of maturity, nurtured by the previous experiences of the natural tourism cluster. The medical tourism cluster role is actually to be innovative, targeting the proposal, tryout and development of products/services intended to cater new segments and/or specific niches.

Thus, keeping the cluster's pipeline with medical tourism products innovations is a vital task that must be coordinated and developed by and within the cluster. Thus, strengthening the role of ProMed is paramount, since its main target is to take advantage of the existing players' synergies in order to reinforce and leverage the ones from the emerging players, so the medical tourism country brand awareness goal could be reached in the middle run.

Within time the cluster cohesion must increase, agglutinating and/ developing more hospitals/clinics/recovery houses/transportation/food and lodging companies, which could align their offering toward the particularities required. The middle service providers (translators, local liaisons, among others) must also, synchronize their efforts with cluster's goal. All the cluster's joint efforts must attract investments from international players, basically in capital intensive infrastructure such as hospitals and clinics. In addition a huge effort is still ahead: in order to drive an increase in demand, which is fully dependable on the willingness of insurance companies in the United States to be serviced by medical tourism providers in Costa Rica and the elimination of legal barriers that are constraining the explosion of a massive demand.

Costa Rica needs to capitalize and leverage on the current top-of-mind possessed internationally, especially amongst the US tourists by developing a consolidated offering of surgery + vacation packages, common feature product of the industry worldwide. The creation of a medical-tourism country brand is likely achievable in less time than the time required by Costa Rica to consolidate its natural tourism country brand, since there is already an extensive know—how of many players, transferable and exploitable by the medical tourism stakeholders. Even when the requirements of the ecotourism/natural products differ from medical tourism products, the learning curve would be shorter for old players such as the Tourism National Department and the Costa Rican Tourism Board. The involvement of other private sector players, providing know-how through their experiences in the past 30 years, is a key element in this development, and the foundation for ProMed to orquestrate and guide the industry development in the near future.

ACKNOWLEDGMENTS

The author thanks Jorge Cortés Rodriguez, MD and General Manager at the Clinica Biblica Hospital, for his unconditional efforts in reviewing and providing feedback to this chapter.

REFERENCES

Alessie, L. (2009). *Medical Tourism: Vaccinated Against the Recession?* Retrieved from HVS website http://www.hvs.com/article/3776/medical-tourism-vaccinated-against-the-recession/. Accessed on April 06, 2013.

Artavia, R., Barahona, J., & Sánchez, J. (1996). *Tourism in costa rica: The challenge to compe-titivity*. Alajuela, Costa Rica: Latin American Center for Competitiveness and Sustainable Development (CLACDS).

Banco Central de la Republica Dominicana. (2013). *Estadisticas Economicas*. Retrieved from http://www.bancentral.gov.do/estadisticas.asp?a=Sector_Real. Accessed on April 13, 2013.

Baudrillard, J. (1968). The system of objects. In M. Poster (Ed.), *Jean Baudrillard: Selected writings*. Cambridge, UK: Polity Press.

Blanke, J., & Chiesa, T. (2011). Executive summary. In J. Blanke & T. Chiesa (Eds.), *The travel & tourism competitiveness report 2011: Beyond the downturn* (pp. xiii–xxvi). Geneva, Switzerland: World Economic Forum.

Blanke, J., Chiesa, T., & Crotti, R. (2013). The travel & tourism competitiveness index 2013: Contributing to national growth and employment. In J. Blanke & T. Chiesa (Eds.), *The travel & tourism competitiveness report 2013: Reducing barriers to economic growth and job creation* (pp. 3–41). Geneva, Switzerland: World Economic Forum.

Butler, R. (1993). Tourism – an evolutionary perspective. In J. G. Nelson, R. W. Butler, & G. Wall (Eds.), *Tourism and sustainable development: Monitoring, planning, and managing* (pp. 24–27). Waterloo, ON: University of Waterloo (Department of Geography Publication 37).

Central America Data. (2013a). *Más turismo médico en Costa Rica*. Retrieved from http://www.centralamericadata.com/es/article/home/Ms_turismo_mdico_en_Costa_Rica. Accessed on April 13, 2013.

Central America Data. (2013b). *La oferta de Costa Rica en turismo medico*. Retrieved from http://www.centralamericadata.com/es/article/home/Costa_Rica_apuesta_a_crecer_en_turismo_mdico. Accessed on April 13, 2013.

Cohen, G. (2010). Protecting patients with passports: Medical tourism and the patient protec-tive-argument. *Iowa Law Review, 95*(5), 1467–1567.

Connell, J. (2006). Sun, sea, sand & … surgery. *Tourism Management, 27*, 1093–1100.

Cook, B. (2009). *Personal interview re. medical tourism opportunities for Costa Rica under the perspective of the medical tourism development department head at the Clinica Blíbica Hospital*. Hospital Clínica Bíblica (Costa Rica), with Rodrigo Murillo, May 28, 2009.

Deloitte. (2008). *Medical tourism. Consumers in search for value*. Washington, DC: Deloitte Center for Health Solutions.

Deloitte. (2009). *Medical tourism: Update and implications*. Washington, DC: Deloitte Center for Health Solutions.

Donald, S. H., & Gammack, J. G. (2007). *Tourism and the branded city: Film and identity on the pacific rim*. Aldershot: Ashgate.

Duar, P. (2009). *Personal interview re. medical tourism under the strategic view of the Costa Rica's General Director of Costa Rican Association for Professionals in Tourism*. ACOPROT (Costa Rican Association for Professionals in Tourism), with Rodrigo Murillo, May 5, 2009.

Euromonitor. (2013). *Costa Rica Quick Stats 2011. Health and Wellness Tourism*. Retrieved from Passport Online Website. Accessed on April 11, 2013.

Future Brand. (2012). *Country Brand Index*. 2013 (8th ed.). Retrieved from http://www.tfsa.ca/storage/reports/CBI_2012-13.pdf. Accessed on March 9, 2013.

Herrick, D. (2007). *Medical Tourism: Global Competition in Health Care*. Policy Report No. 304. National Center for Policy Analysis. Dallas, Texas.

Herrick, D. (2008). *Medical Tourism: Health Care Free Trade.* Policy Report No. 623. National Center for Policy Analysis, Dallas, TX. Retrieved from http://www.ncpa.org/pub/ba623. Accessed on April 8, 2013.

Inman, C., Mesa, N., Flores, K., & Prado, A. (2002). *Tourism in Costa Rica: The Challenge of Competitiveness.* Working Paper. Latin American Center for Competitiveness and Sustainable Development (CLACDS). Alajuela, Costa Rica.

Instituto Costarricense de Turismo. (2007). *Plan Nacional de Turismo Sostenible de Costa Rica 2002–2012, Actualización 2006.* Instituto Costarricense de Turismo.

Instituto Costarricense de Turismo. (2010). *Plan Nacional de Turismo Sostenible de Costa Rica 2010–2016,* Instituto Costarricense de Turismo.

Instituto Costarricense de Turismo. (2012). *Tourism Statistical Yearly Report 2011,* Costa Rica.

JICA, & ICT – Agencia de Cooperación Internacional del Japón and Instituto Costarricense de Turismo – (2001). *Estudio para el Plan de Uso de la Tierra en las Zonas Costeras de las unidades de Planeamiento Turístico en la República de Costa Rica. Final Report* (Vol 3). Pacific Consultants Internacional. Yachiyo Engineering Co. Ltd.

Little, I. (2010). The Ramada is doing it right – a blueprint to follow when catering to medical tourists. 11 May 2010. *Espace Artist. Medical Tourism Online.* Retrieved from http://medicaltourism.escapeartist.com/resources-medical/the-ramada-is-doing-it-right-%E2%80%93-a-blueprint-to-follow-when-catering-to-medical-tourists/. Accessed on March 12, 2013.

Manzi, M. (2009). *Personal interview re. medical tourism under the strategic view of the Costa Rica's Minister of Competitiveness Assessor.* Ministry of Competitiveness of Costa Rica, with Rodrigo Murillo, May 29, 2009.

Medical Tourism. (2013). Surgeries Cost Comparison. *Medical Tourism website.* Retrieved from http://www.medicaltourism.com/en/compare-costs.html. Accessed on June 12, 2013.

Morgan, N., Pritchard, A., & Pride, R. (Eds.). (2002). *Destination branding: Creating the unique destination proposition.* Boston: Butterworth-Heinemann.

Murillo, R., Kilian, B., & Castro, R. (2011). Chapter 12. Leveraging and sustainability of PES. In B. Rapidel, F. DeClerck, J. Le Coq, & J. Beer (Eds.), *Lessons learned in Costa Rica ecosystem services from agriculture and agroforestry measurement and payment* (pp. 267–287). London: Earthscan.

National Institute of Dental and Craniofacial Research. (2013). *Oral Health in America: A Report of the Surgeon General (Executive Summary).* Retrieved from http://www.nidcr.nih.gov/datastatistics/surgeongeneral/report/executivesummary.htm. Accessed on April 8, 2013.

Pacific Prime. (2012). *The top 10 medical tourism destinations in 2012 so far* International Health Insurance Online. Retrieved from http://www.pacificprime.com/blog/the-top-10-medical-tourism-destinations-in-2012-so-far.html. Accessed on April 12, 2013.

Piazolo, M., & Zanca, N. (2011). Medical tourism – A case study for the USA and India, Germany and Hungary. *Acta Polytechnica Hungary, 8,* 27–38.

Plunkett Research. (2013). *Health Expenditures and Services in the U.S.* Retrieved from http://www.plunkettresearch.com/health-care-medical-market-research/industry-trends. Accessed on April 06, 2013.

Richter, M. (2012). *Medical tourism sets pulses racing. Agence France-Presse (AFP).* Retrieved from http://www.google.com/hostednews/afp/article/ALeqM5jD_0iy7v_HpPicSMm JFWq04iGBg?docId=CNG.f06b3f115da0bd54c843b2d1d70de8f8.8f1. Accessed on April 12, 2013.

Rosenthal, J. (2009). Medical tourism takes off. *National Geographic Traveler, 26*, 10−16.

Skyscanner. (2009). Nature Holidays in World's 10 Greenest Countries. Retrieved from http://www.skyscanner.net/news/nature-holidays-world-s-10-greenest-countries. Accessed on March 9, 2013.

The Medica. (2013). *Medical Industry Overview*. Retrieved from http://www.themedica.com/industry-overview.html. Accessed on April 06, 2013.

United Nations Development Program. (2009). *Human Development Report 2009 Overcoming barriers: Human mobility and development*. Canada: Lowe−Martin Group.

United Nations World Tourism Organization. (2009). *UNWTO World Tourism Barometer*, Interim Update, April 3, 2009.

Valentine, P. (1992). Review: Nature-based tourism. In: *Special interest tourism* (pp. 105−127). London, Great Britain: Belhaven Press.

Wood, M. (2002). *Ecotourism: Principles, practices & policies for sustainability* (1st ed.). Paris, France: United Nations Environmental Program, Division of Technology Industry and Economics, Production Unit, United Nations Publications.

World Health Organization. (2012). *World health statistics 2012*. Geneva, Switzerland: WHO Library Cataloguing-in-Publication Data.

Yanos, M. (2008). *Top 5 Medical Tourism Destinations. Medical tourism can mean attractive opportunities for foreign patients and investors*. NuWire Investor Online. Retrieved from http://www.nuwireinvestor.com/articles/top-5-medical-tourism-destinations-51502.aspx. Accessed on April 12, 2013.

CHAPTER 8

DESTINATION BRAND PERFORMANCE MEASUREMENT OVER TIME

Steven Pike

ABSTRACT

With increasing investments being made in brand development by destination marketing organisations (DMO) since the 1990s, including rebranding and repositioning, more research is necessary to enhance understanding of how to effectively monitor destination brand performance over time. This chapter summarises key findings from a study of brand performance of a competitive set of destinations, in their most important market, between 2003 and 2012. Brand performance was measured from the perspective of consumer perceptions, based on the concept of consumer-based brand equity (CBBE). The results indicated almost no change in perceptions of the five destinations over the 10-year period. Due to the commonality of challenges faced by DMOs worldwide, it is suggested the CBBE hierarchy provides destination marketers with a practical tool for evaluating brand performance over time; in terms of

Tourists' Perceptions and Assessments
Advances in Culture, Tourism and Hospitality Research, Volume 8, 111–120
ISSN: 1871-3173/doi:10.1108/S1871-317320140000008005

measures of effectiveness of past marketing communications, as well as indicators of future performance.

Keywords: Destination image; destination branding; destination marketing

INTRODUCTION

While case studies have shown that destinations can be branded by DMOs (see e.g. Morgan, Pritchard, & Piggott, 2002), few studies report on the analysis of consumer perceptions of destination brand performance over time. This temporal aspect is an important gap in the literature, given (i) the increasing investments being made in branding initiatives by destination marketing organisations (DMO) since the 1990s, which have included rebranding and repositioning attempts, and (ii) the proposition three decades ago that destination image change will only occur slowly over time (Gartner & Hunt, 1987).

In Queensland, Australia, 13 regional tourism organisations (RTO) are officially recognised by the state tourism organisation (STO), Tourism Queensland (see www.tq.com.au). The STO provides financial and human resource assistance to the RTOs, much of which has been invested in the development of destination brand campaigns. Brisbane, the state capital, is the most important market in terms of visitor arrivals for most destinations in Queensland. In this project the destination of interest is the Coral Coast, which has been categorised by Tourism Queensland as an 'emerging destination'. In 2002, Tourism Queensland undertook a series of focus groups with Brisbane residents to investigate perceptions of the Bundaberg region, and found the area lacked a clear identity as a tourism destination. A new destination brand, developed by the RTO and STO was launched in 2003 with the objectives being: (i) to raise awareness of the destination, (ii) to stimulate increased interest in, and visitation to the region and (iii) educate the market about things to do. In 2003, this research commenced to benchmark perceptions of the destination, relative to competing regions, in the Brisbane market, immediately prior to the campaign launch. The aim was to monitor effectiveness of the brand over time, relative to the three objectives, which would provide performance effectiveness measures to the DMO. Two further studies were undertaken in 2007 and 2012.

THEORETICAL CONSIDERATIONS

The topic of branding first appeared in the marketing literature over 60 years ago (see Banks, 1950). However, the tourism destination branding literature did not commence until 1998 (see Dosen, Vransevic, & Prebezac, 1998). In the time since, this emergent field has attracted increasing academic interest, with a recent review by Pike (2009) tabling 74 publications by 102 authors published between 1998 and 2007. However, there has been a lack of research published in relation to the temporal aspect of destination brand performance. This chapter reports a rare investigation into the measurement of perceptions of destination brands over a 10-year period. The findings of the study suggest desired changes in induced destination image, through marketing communications by destination marketing organisations (DMO), will probably only occur slowly over a long period of time. The study measured destination brand performance using the consumer-based brand equity hierarchy promoted by Aaker (1991, 1996).

For consumer goods firms, the concept of *brand equity* is commonly used as an indicator of performance, and is reported as a financial value on the corporate balance sheet. However, such an intangible asset value of the brand will be of little practical use to DMOs and their stakeholders. Another tool in brand effectiveness measurement that is better suited to DMOs is consumer-based brand equity (CBBE). Destination CBBE is conceptualised in this project as the function of a hierarchy of brand salience, brand associations and brand loyalty. Recent structural equation modelling has demonstrated the relationships between these three constructs (see Bianchi & Pike, 2011; Konecknik & Gartner, 2007).

Brand salience is at the foundation of the CBBE hierarchy, and represents the strength of the destination's presence in the mind of the consumer when a given travel situation is being considered. Using the theory of consumer decision sets a number of studies have supported the assertion that the number of destinations a traveller will actually consider in the purchase process is limited to four plus or minus two (see e.g. Pike & Ryan, 2004; Woodside & Lysonski, 1989; Woodside & Sherrell, 1977). Destinations not positioned in the consumer's decision set are not salient, and are therefore at a competitive disadvantage. This CBBE dimension relates to the DMOs first brand objective: 'To increase awareness of the destination'. Brand associations are anything linked in memory to the destination. This CBBE dimension relates to the DMOs second objective: 'To educate the market about things to do'. Reviews of the extensive destination image literature (see Gallarza, Saura, & Garcia, 2002; Pike, 2002) no commonly agreed conceptualisation of the construct exists, and therefore no accepted scale index.

Mayo and Jarvis (1981) propose an individual would make a brand selection based on what is 'important and relevant to them' (p. 68), and so associations need to be measured in terms of attributes deemed determinant to individuals for a given travel situation. Determinacy represents those features relating most closely to purchase decisions. Brand loyalty, the highest level of the hierarchy, and is related to the destination's third objective: 'To stimulate interest in, and visitation to, the destination'. The topic of destination loyalty has been neglected until relatively recently. This construct can be measured by attitudinal loyalty, such as stated intent to visit, and word of mouth recommendations, and/or behavioural loyalty such as actual repeat visitation.

METHOD

The initial 2003 study was a longitudinal design, using a systematic random sample drawn from the Brisbane telephone directory. The first stage questionnaire contained questions about recent and intended short break holiday activity, ToMA/decision set preferences, and importance ratings of a battery of short break destination attributes. The second questionnaire, distributed to the same participants three months later, involved questions about actual travel undertaken since the first questionnaire, and perceptions of the competitive set of five destinations across the battery of attributes. The 2007 study used a different sample, randomly drawn from an updated Brisbane telephone directory, and again a mail questionnaire was used. The 2012 study used a new sample invited from the panel of a commercial marketing research firm, and the questionnaire was administered online. The questionnaire used in 2007 and 2012 consisted of 173 items in three sections. The first section included filter questions about attitudes towards short breaks, two unaided questions to elicit the top of mind awareness (ToMA) destination and decision set composition, and a battery of 22 destination attribute-importance items using a seven point scale (1 = not important, 7 = very important).

The attribute list was developed from a review of the literature, practitioner opinion, and personal interviews with Brisbane residents. A 'don't know' option was also provided for each scale item. These attributes were selected from the results of the 2003 study, supplemented by attributes from further exploratory research using group applications of the Repertory Test with Brisbane residents. The second section asked participants to rate the perceived performance of the Coral Coast, along with four competing destinations selected from the decision set findings of the 2003 study, across the 22 cognitive scale items, and two affective scale items. Questions were also used to identify measures of previous visitation, intent to visit and word of mouth recommendations for each of the five destinations.

FINDINGS

The useable sample sizes were 521 in 2003, 444 in 2007 and 541 in 2012. Participants indicated a strong familiarity with short break holidays, with a mean of three such trips by car per year in 2003 and 2007, and 2.5 in 2012.

Destination Brand Salience

The unaided brand salience question elicited over 100 preferred ToMA destinations from participants in 2003, 2007 and 2012. For reporting succinctness the list has been categorised in Table 1 by RTO geographic boundary. The ranking of each destination was consistent between 2003, 2007 and 2012. The mean number of destinations listed in decision sets was 3.8 in 2003, 3.1 in 2007 and 2.6 in 2012, all within the theorised range of 4+/−2. The 2003 longitudinal study identified a relationship between destinations listed in decision sets and actual travel.

Table 1. Destination Brand Salience.

Destination	2003		2007		2012	
	n	%	n	%	n	%
Sunshine Coast	231	45.1	202	45.9	174	32.2
Gold Coast	96	18.8	72	16.4	110	20.3
Northern NSW	57	11.1	64	14.5	65	12.0
Fraser Coast	33	6.4	24	5.5	25	4.6
Coral Coast	11	2.1	6	1.4	10	1.8
Other	84	16.5	72	16.3	157	29
Missing	11		7			
Total	**523**		**447**		**541**	

Therefore, the decision set size and composition has serious implications for those destinations not listed, such as the Coral Coast, since these destinations are less likely to be considered in the selection process. Coral Coast destinations were listed in 58 (11%) participants' decision sets in the 2003 study, 25 (6%) in 2007, and 20 (4%) in 2012. The ToMA and decision set findings highlight a lack of improvement in *brand salience* for the Coral Coast between 2003 and 2012. This is important given brand salience is the foundation of the CBBE hierarchy, and was the RTOs first objective for the new brand campaign.

Destination Brand Associations

In relation to the RTOs second objective, Table 2 shows the brand associations for the Coral Coast did not improve across any of the cognitive and affective items over the 10-year period. However, with the exception of three attributes, the means for the cognitive items were at least favourably higher than the scale midpoint. From a positioning perspective, the Coral Coast consistently rated lowest on half of the cognitive items and both affective items, but highest on three attributes. It is suggested that two of these, 'friendly locals' and 'uncrowded', represent an as yet unused market position that the RTO could better exploit in marketing communications. As mentioned, a 'don't know' option was provided alongside each of the cognitive attribute scale items. For the attribute-importance items, the maximum rate of 'don't know' usage was 1.3%, which indicated participants were familiar with the attributes. However, every Coral Coast performance item attracted a 'don't know' non-response rate of between 30% and 50%. For the Coral Coast RTO, the implication is that more work is needed to improve cognition of what the destination has to offer.

Destination Brand Loyalty

In terms of brand loyalty, over 90% of participants had previously visited their unaided ToMA destination in 2003, 2007 and 2012. While 40% of participants indicated having previously visited the Coral Coast, the mean likelihood of visiting the Coral Coast within the next year was 2.7, which showed no improvement from 2003 or 2007. An indicator of possible future performance, this was the lowest of the competitive set of destinations, as it was in 2003 and 2007. Participants were asked to rate the extent to which

Table 2. Brand Associations for the Coral Coast.

	2003		2007		2012	
	Mean	Rank	Mean	Rank	Mean	Rank
Pleasant climate	5.9	4	5.8	4 =	5.4	4 =
Uncrowded	5.6	1	5.0	1 =	4.4	1 =
Not touristy	5.6	1	4.6	1	4.3	1
Good value for money	5.5	2 =	5.1	2 =	4.7	3 =
A safe destination	5.5	4	5.4	3	5.1	3
Places for walking	5.4	4	4.5	4	4.5	4
Friendly locals	5.4	2 =	5.2	1	4.8	3
Suitable accommodation	5.2	5	5.1	5	5.0	5
Lots to see and do	5.0	5	5.0	5	4.7	5
Good beaches	5.1	5	5.1	5	4.8	5
High levels of service	4.9	4	4.4	5	4.3	5
Good cafes and restaurants	4.7	4	4.4	4 =	4.3	5
Within a comfortable drive	3.6	5	3.8	5	3.6	5
Affordable packages	–	–	4.9	2	4.5	4
Beautiful scenery	–	–	5.6	4	5.2	4
Places for swimming	–	–	5.3	5	5.0	5
Family destination	–	–	5.4	3	4.9	3 =
Good shopping	–	–	4.0	4	3.8	4
Historical places	–	–	4.6	1	4.4	1
Marine life	–	–	5.3	2 =	5.0	3
Trendy atmosphere	–	–	3.5	5	3.6	5
Water sports	–	–	4.7	5	4.6	5
Affective benefits						
Sleepy/arousing	3.8	5	3.7	5	3.6	5
Unpleasant/pleasant	5.0	5	4.7	5	4.3	4

they would recommend each destination to friends. On this seven point scale (1 = definitely not, 7 = definitely) the mean for the Coral Coast was 3.9 in 2007 and 3.7 in 2012. This result, which was not measured in 2003, was the lowest of the five destinations.

CONCLUSION AND IMPLICATIONS

Research is lacking in the tourism literature relating to the temporal aspect of consumer perceptions of destinations, since the early work of Gartner and Hunt (1987). This is an important issue in this project given the purpose of the research was the image problem faced by the destination and the RTO's development of a new brand to change market perceptions. It has been suggested that while individual components of a destination's image may fluctuate greatly over time, their effect on overall image might not be influential. Gartner and Hunt (1987) provide evidence of positive destination image change over a 13-year period, but conclude that any change only occurs slowly. Likewise, Anholt's national brand index (see Anholt, 2010, p. 6) has shown that nation image is a 'remarkably stable phenomenon'. There have been few research papers demonstrating how DMOs have been able to successfully rebrand and reposition their destination. It is suggested the CBBE hierarchy outlined above has the potential to provide *one* means by which DMOs could transparently demonstrate accountability, by generating and publishing data that measures the outcomes of branding objectives.

One of the problems in destination branding practice that has been highlighted previously is that too many destination brand positioning themes have been less than memorable, with best practise limited to a few simple slogans such as 'I ♥ New York'. A key issue has been the lack of longevity in so many campaigns. For example, in the United States, of 47 state slogans used by US STOs in 1982 (see Pritchard, 1982) only 6 were in use in 1993 (see Richardson & Cohen, 1993), and of those slogans being used in 1993, only 13 were still being used in 2003 (see Pike, 2004).

To differentiate a destination from competing places offering similar features, DMOs are increasingly engaging in place branding. The purpose of the chapter was to report the results of the tracking of destination branding performance over time. Other than Curtis' (2001) analysis of the development of Oregon's brand during the 1980s and 1990s, there have been few temporal analyses of the effectiveness of destination brands. In this chapter, a hierarchy of CBBE was trialled as a means of measuring the effectiveness three key universal DMO objectives. Destination marketing takes place in a political environment, with DMO staff accountable to government funding agencies, local tourism businesses, travel intermediaries and the host community. Pressure to justify the brand rationale and to change brand initiatives can be exerted by such stakeholders. CBBE provides destination marketers with a useful tool to guide stakeholders on brand objectives, in addition to offering a practical and structured approach towards measuring performance of brand positioning.

For the Coral Coast, the structure of the results provide measures of brand salience, brand associations, and brand loyalty in the destination's most important market, in the context of short breaks by car, after 10 years of a new brand campaign. The CBBE structure provides indicators, related to the brand campaign objectives, for which the effectiveness of future promotional activity can be evaluated. The results highlighted a positioning opportunity that has not yet been exploited by the destination. These attributes could be used more explicitly in future brand promotions, since the easiest route to the mind is to reinforce positively held perceptions rather than to attempt to try to change opinions (see Ries & Trout, 1982).

Overall, the results support the assertion by Gartner and Hunt (1987) that destination image change will only take place over a long period of time. This conclusion has serious implications for destination marketers considering changing brand positioning themes. The important issue of accountability of the DMO to their stakeholders warrants more attention in the literature. In relation to branding, one of the greatest challenges lies in harnessing stakeholders' cooperation in collaboratively supporting the brand positioning required to communicate the brand identity (Anholt, 2010). To date research is scarce about the extent to which DMOs and stakeholders adhere to this tenet.

REFERENCES

Aaker, D. A. (1991). *Managing brand equity*. New York, NY: Free Press.

Aaker, D. A. (1996). *Building strong brands*. New York, NY: Free Press.

Anholt, S. (2010). *Places: Identity, image and reputation*. Basingstoke, Hampshire: MacMillan.

Banks, S. (1950). The relationships between preference and purchase of brands. *Journal of Marketing, 15*(2), 145–157.

Bianchi, C., & Pike, S. (2011). Antecedents of attitudinal destination loyalty in a long-haul market: Australia's brand equity among Chilean consumers. *Journal of Travel & Tourism Marketing, 28*(7), 736–750.

Curtis, J. (2001). Branding a state: The evolution of brand Oregon. *Journal of Vacation Marketing, 7*(1), 75–81.

Dosen, D. O., Vranesevic, T., & Prebezac, D. (1998). The importance of branding in the development of marketing strategy of Croatia as tourist destination. *ActaTuristica, 10*(2), 93–182.

Gallarza, M. G., Saura, I. G., & Garcia, H. C. (2002). Destination image: Toward a conceptual framework. *Annals of Tourism Research, 29*(1), 56–78.

Gartner, W. C., & Hunt, J. D. (1987). An analysis of state image change over a twelve-year period (1971–1983). *Journal of Travel Research, 26*(2), 15–19.

Konecknik, M., & Gartner, W. C. (2007). Customer-based brand equity for a destination. *Annals of Tourism Research, 34*(2), 400–421.

Mayo, E. J., & Jarvis, L. P. (1981). *The psychology of leisure travel*. Massachusetts: CBI Publishing.

Morgan, N. J., Pritchard, A., & Piggott, R. (2002). New Zealand, 100% pure. The creation of a powerful niche destination brand. *Journal of Brand Management, 9*(4–5), 335–354.

Pike, S. (2002). Destination image analysis: A review of 142 papers from 1973–2000. *Tourism Management, 23*(5), 541–549.

Pike, S. (2004). Destination brand positioning slogans – Towards the development of a set of accountability criteria. *Acta Turistica, 16*(2), 102–124.

Pike, S. (2009). Destination brand positions of a competitive set of near-home destinations. *Tourism Management, 30*(6), 857–866.

Pike, S., & Ryan, C. (2004). Destination positioning analysis through a comparison of cognitive, affective and conative perceptions. *Journal of Travel Research, 42*(4), 333–342.

Pritchard, G. (1982). Tourism promotion: Big business for the states. *Cornell Quarterly, 23*(2), 48–57.

Richardson, J., & Cohen, J. (1993). State slogans: The case of the missing USP. *Journal of Travel and Tourism Marketing, 2*(2–3), 91–109.

Ries, A., & Trout, J. (1982). The enormous competitive power of a selling product name. *Marketing Times, 29*(5), 28–38.

Woodside, A. G., & Lysonski, S. (1989). A general model of traveler destination choice. *Journal of Travel Research, 27*(4), 8–14.

Woodside, A. G., & Sherrell, D. (1977). Traveler evoked, inept, and inert sets of vacation destinations. *Journal of Travel Research, 16*, 14–18.

CHAPTER 9

PERCEPTIONS OF HOTEL DISINTERMEDIATION: THE FRENCH GENERATION Y CASE

Girish Prayag and Giacomo Del Chiappa

ABSTRACT

Generation Y is a new sizable market that is fast changing as the landscape of the internet rapidly evolves. Until now, research has examined mainly the perceptions of different online buyers of accommodation in specific geographical areas, with little attention devoted to Generation Y. This study examines Generation Y travelers' perceptions of hotel disintermediation in France. The results, based on a sample of 378 French travelers, show four underlying dimensions of perceptions. Findings also reveal that only gender and age significantly influence perceptions. The chapter closes with implications for increasing trust and attractiveness of the online accommodation offer to French Generation Y.

Keywords: Disintermediation; user generated content; socio-demographics; generation Y; France

Tourists' Perceptions and Assessments
Advances in Culture, Tourism and Hospitality Research, Volume 8, 121–127
Copyright © 2014 by Emerald Group Publishing Limited
All rights of reproduction in any form reserved
ISSN: 1871-3173/doi:10.1108/S1871-317320140000008006

INTRODUCTION

The rapidly evolving landscape of the internet has reshaped the way people plan for, buy and consume tourism products and services (Buhalis & Law, 2008; Xiang & Gretzel, 2010). Specifically, user generated content (UCG) and "Travel 2.0" applications are amongst the most important sources of information for consumers making an online purchasing decision (Gretzel & Yoo, 2008). Inevitably, the internet has dramatically changed the role of tourism intermediaries (Kracht & Wang, 2009) and transformed the tourism value chain (Berne, Garcia-Gonzalez, & Mugica, 2012). Yet, existing studies mostly examine online information search behavior, online benefits to travelers and marketers, and online concerns and opportunities (Jang, 2004). Limited studies examine how the demographic profile of online travelers influences travel planning behavior (Ip, Lee, & Law, 2012) and the online behavior of Generation Y (Bolton et al., 2013; Nusair, Parsa, & Cobanoglu, 2011).

Generation Y is considered a new sizable market (Bolton et al., 2013; Sullivan & Heitmeyer, 2008) for online service providers given young consumers' buying power and immersion in online behaviors. Generation Y is usually defined as those people born between 1978 and 1994 (Sheahan, 2009). The global travel spending of Generation Y is worth $136 billion annually (WTO, 2008) and this generation tends to use the internet for 15% of their purchases (Sullivan & Heitmeyer, 2008). The limited studies on Generation Y focus mostly on the social-media usage patterns (Bolton et al., 2013). Generation Y perceptions of the hotel offer online compared to traditional travel agencies offer remain under researched (Del Chiappa, 2013a, 2013b).

Hence, the main objectives of this study are to examine the perceptions of Generation Y on hotel disintermediation in France; and to assess the influence of demographics on such perceptions. "Disintermediation" is the idea that the role of the middleman will diminish or be eliminated as consumers turn more to online service providers (Buhalis, 1998).

By doing so, the contribution of the study is twofold. First, the extent of disintermediation perceived by Generation Y is an important issue. Of French consumers accessing the internet, 37% were doing so for travel-related services, which is marginally higher than the European average of 35% (Eurostat Statistical Books, 2010). Of these consumers, the age group 15−24 years old is very active in the search for travel-related services (Cabinet Raffour Interactif, 2011). Second, the influence of demographics on consumer online behaviors has been sparsely examined (Ip et al., 2012). Contradictory evidence exists on the influence of age, gender and education level on online behaviors (Belonda, 2005; Ip et al., 2012).

THEORETICAL CONSIDERATIONS

Arguments exist for and against disintermediation of the tourism distribution channel (Buhalis, 1998; Law, 2009). Among the arguments in favor of disintermediation, include the great flexibility and variety of consumer choice made possible by internet, the poor level of training and competence of travel agency personnel and the fact that travel agencies are biased towards suppliers who offer overriding commissions (Buhalis, 1998).

On the other hand, arguments against disintermediation include for example, the time saving that travel agencies grant their customers, the human touch they provide, and the reduction in uncertainty and insecurity they ensure by assuming the responsibility for all arrangements (Buhalis, 1998). Factors differentiating online customers of hotel reservation and non-online customers include, convenience, ease of information search and transaction, information credibility, price and safety (Kim & Kim, 2004). The French market typically uses the internet as a source of information rather than a purchase option for travel-related products (CCM Benchmark, 2010). The role of the traditional travel agent is seemingly one of continued importance in the French travel market.

"Lookers" differ from "bookers" in several socio-demographic characteristics and in their internet usage. Lookers are consumers who use the internet to acquire information while bookers are those who also use it to buy tourism services and products. Some studies suggest that the propensity to purchase online increases with age, education level, and income (Law, Leung, & Wong, 2004). Others (e.g., Belonda, 2005) found that the propensity to use the internet for information search is higher among older cohorts in the United States than younger cohorts. Except for age, gender, and education level cannot distinguish between online and non-online customers of hotel reservation, with older customers more likely to book hotels online (Kim & Kim, 2004). To the contrary, Ip et al. (2012) observe that age, education level and income influence the use of travel websites for travel planning and that users are typically young, highly educated, and have high personal income.

METHOD

The survey instrument captures the online buying behavior of young travelers. Travelers' usage patterns of online hotel reservation and traditional travel agencies are assessed using questions adapted from Del Chiappa (2013a, 2013b). The survey instrument also measures 16 statements related to perceptions of online booking and the use of traditional travel agencies on a five-point Likert scale (1 = Strongly Disagree and 5 = Strongly Agree), adapted from the following studies (Buhalis, 1998; Del Chiappa, 2013a, 2013b; Kim & Kim, 2004; Law, 2009). The use of the internet for different types of pleasure travel at different geographical scale (national, regional, and international), length of the trip (short vs. medium/long) is also measured along with various socio-demographics. The survey instrument was available in two languages, English and French.

Using a self-completion method, the survey targeted mainly undergraduate and postgraduate students at the largest private French Business School. The location offers an environment conducive for identification of Generation Y travelers, given that the general profile of young online buyers is one of relatively high socio-economic status and having unfettered access to information technology and social-media platforms (Bolton et al., 2013). Using a convenience sample, 378 useable questionnaires were obtained. More than half (56.3%) of the respondents surveyed were female. The age bracket 18−25 years old was the largest (81%). The sample was well educated with 39.5% holding university degrees and 34.9% having completed high school.

RESULTS

Young travelers in general are mostly neutral toward the role of travel agencies in providing services that they value for accommodation booking. For example, they perceive travel agents as professional counselors ($M = 3.39$) who are able to understand the needs of their customers ($M = 3.53$), thus being able to provide a better service in terms of human touch ($M = 3.38$), personalization ($M = 3.44$), and reduction of booking insecurity ($M = 3.66$). Travel agents are perceived also as being business minded, placing their financial incentives before the interests and needs of their customers ($M = 3.48$). However, perceptions of the internet as a source of information and booking tool are mostly positive. For example, they agree about the time saving (M = 4.18) and convenience (M = 4.18) aspects of internet booking for hotel reservation.

To better understand the underlying dimensions of disintermediation perceptions, the 16 items are factor analyzed yielding four factors explaining 52% of the variance. The factors are labeled: F1 − Benefits of Online Reservation; F2 − Benefits of Travel Agency; F3 − Online Trust & Search Behavior; and F4 − Transaction Costs of Travel Agency. The Cronbach's alphas indicate internal consistency for most factors. Accordingly, four summated scales are created to identify the influence of demographics on the factors. T-tests reveal that gender has a significant influence on F1 (t = −0.778, p < 0.05), whereby females (M = 3.95) are slightly more agreeable than males (M = 3.84) on the benefits of using the Internet for hotel reservation. Age has a significant influence on F4 (t = 11.23, p < 0.01), whereby the younger Gen Y (18−25 years old) has (M = 3.38) marginally higher agreement levels compared to older Gen Y (26−35 years old) (M = 3.32) on travel agents charging high transaction costs.

CONCLUSION AND IMPLICATIONS

The findings provide insights on the perceptions of the extent of disintermediation in the French tourism and travel industry. The findings have both theoretical and managerial implications. Young French travelers are heavy users of internet as a tool for both searching and booking hotels. These findings contradict the perception that the French have historically a high level of reliance on travel agencies (Sabre Travel Network, 2011). Generation Y seems to have a different online behavior. However, the influence of socio-demographics on perceptions is rather mitigated. While age has a significant influence on perceptions as other studies suggest (Ip et al., 2012; Kim & Kim, 2004), education level has no impact. Surprisingly, gender has an influence on perceptions in contrast to other studies (Kim & Kim, 2004), perhaps explainable by cultural differences between the French and the rest of Europe.

The findings suggest that online hotel marketers fair better than traditional travel agencies. For continued success, online providers of accommodation should increase the attractiveness of their websites and making young travelers' feel a sense of belonging to the hotel. Indeed, recent research showed that affective commitment is the most effective for developing and maintaining mutually beneficial relationships with Generation Y

(Nusair et al., 2011). To reach this goal, hoteliers can use several strategies such as, increase the emphasis on personalization and playfulness online in order to make the shopping experiences more enjoyable and more indulging, facilitating online communities, providing better service quality, and offering faster responses to customer suggestions and complaints (Nusair et al., 2011). Travel agents on the other hand should create and maintain a presence online and should enhance their competence in behaving as professional counselors in order to create more positive perceptions of their offer among Generation Y.

The generalization of this research is limited by its method of sampling (i.e., convenience sample) but offers insights into disintermediation and UGC, contextualizing the findings on French Generation Y. Future studies should examine whether different segments of young travelers are identifiable based on their perceptions of disintermediation. Likewise, investigating disintermediation in other European countries for the same generation, adopting an information search perspective, and making a distinction between information sources and information channels could be other avenues for research in this area.

REFERENCES

Belonda, S. (2005). Cohort analysis of online travel information search behavior: 1995−2000. *Journal of Travel Research, 44*(Nov), 135−142.

Berne, C., Garcia-Gonzalez, M., & Mugica, J. (2012). How ICT shifts the power balance of tourism distribution channels. *Tourism Management, 33*(1), 205−214.

Bolton, R. N., Parasuraman, A., Hoefnagels, A., Migchels, N., Kabadayi, S., Gruber, T., Loureiro, Y. K., & Solnet, D. (2013). Understanding generation Y and their use of social media: A review and research agenda. *Journal of Service Management, 24*(3), 245−267.

Buhalis, D. (1998). Strategic use of information technologies in the tourism industry. *Tourism Management, 19*(5), 409−421.

Buhalis, D., & Law, R. (2008). Progress in information technology and tourism management: 20 years on and 10 years after the internet − The state of eTourism research. *Tourism Management, 29*(4), 609−623.

Cabinet Raffour Interactif. (2011). *Baromètre Courts Séjours, Vacances, Nouvelles Tendances et e-Tourisme*. Paris: Raffour.

CCM Benchmark. (2010). France: le marché du tourisme en ligne. Retrieved from http://journaldunet.com/cc/10_tourisme. Accessed on March 13, 2012.

Del Chiappa, G. (2013a). Internet versus travel agencies: The perception of different groups of Italian online buyers. *Journal of Vacation Marketing, 19*(1), 1−12.

Del Chiappa, G. (2013b). Italian online buyers' perceptions of the topic of disintermediation and user generated content. In M. Kozack & N. Kozack (Eds.), *Aspects of tourist behavior*. Newcastle, UK: Cambridge Scholars Publishing.

Eurostat Statistical Books. (2010). More than half of internet users post messages to social media. Retrieved from http://epp.eurostat.ec.europa.eu/cache/. Accessed on April 13, 2012.

Gretzel, U., & Yoo, K. H. (2008). Use and impact of online travel reviews. In P. O'Connor, W. Höpken, & U. Gretzel (Eds.), *Information and Communication Technologies in Tourism proceedings of the international conference in Innsbruck*, Austria, 2008 (pp. 35–46). Vienna: Springer-Verlag.

Ip, C., Lee, H. A., & Law, R. (2012). Profiling users of travel websites for planning and online experience sharing. *Journal of Hospitality & Tourism Research, 36*(3), 418–426.

Jang, S. S. (2004). The past, present, and future research of online information search. *Journal of Travel & Tourism Marketing, 17*(2–3), 41–47.

Kim, W. G., & Kim, D. J. (2004). Factors affecting online hotel reservation intention between online and non-online customers. *International Journal of Hospitality Management, 23*, 381–385.

Kracht, J., & Wang, Y. (2009). Examining the tourism distribution channel: Evolution and transformation. *International Journal of Contemporary Hospitality Management, 22*(5), 736–757.

Law, R. (2009). Disintermediation of hotel reservations: The perception of different groups of online buyers in Hong Kong. *International Journal of Contemporary Hospitality Management, 21*(6), 766–772.

Law, R., Leung, K., & Wong, J. (2004). The impact of the Internet on travel agencies. *International Journal of Contemporary Hospitality Management, 16*(2), 100–107.

Nusair, K. K., Parsa, H. G., & Cobanoglu, C. (2011). Building a model of commitment for generation Y: An empirical study on e-travel retailers. *Tourism Management, 32*(4), 833–843.

Sabre Travel Network. (2011). European Online Travel Agencies: Navigating New Challenges: Intelligence Report by PhoCusWright: US.

Sheahan, P. (2009). *Gen Y: Thriving and surviving with gen Y at work*. New York, NY: Hardie Grant Books.

Sullivan, P., & Heitmeyer, J. (2008). Looking at gen Y shopping preferences and intentions: Exploring the role of experience and apparel involvement. *International Journal of Consumer Studies, 32*(3), 285–295.

World Tourism Organization. (2008). Youth travel matter. Understanding the Global Phenomenon of Youth Travel. Report by the WTO. Madrid: Spain.

Xiang, Z., & Gretzel, U. (2010). Role of social media in online travel information search. *Tourism Management, 31*, 179–188.

CHAPTER 10

CONSTRUCTING AND SHAPING TOURIST EXPERIENCES VIA TRAVEL BLOG ENGAGEMENT

Nik Alia Wan Ab Rahman, Sangkyun Kim and Steve Brown

ABSTRACT

This chapter aims to develop a holistic conceptual understanding of how tourism experiences are constructed, contextualized and packaged in the context of travel blogs. Tourist experiences are highlighted as an on-going process, continuously changing and altering during pre-, on-site-, and post-visit of tourist experiences. This chapter also examines the relationships between travel blog users' motivation and engagement and tourist experience construction. As a result, a new dimension to the previous tourist experiences is offered.

Keywords: Travel blog; motivation; engagement; tourist experience; social media

Tourists' Perceptions and Assessments
Advances in Culture, Tourism and Hospitality Research, Volume 8, 129–135
Copyright © 2014 by Emerald Group Publishing Limited
All rights of reproduction in any form reserved
ISSN: 1871-3173/doi:10.1108/S1871-317320140000008007

INTRODUCTION

While some studies investigate the role of social media in travel planning and information searching at the pre-visit stage of tourist experiences (Cox, Burgess, Sellitto, & Buultjens, 2009; Xiang & Gretzel, 2010), others examine the influence of social media on en-route information searching and decision making during traveling at the on-site stage (Fotis, Buhalis, & Rossides, 2011; Jun, Hartwell, & Buhalis, 2012). The post-visit stage of tourist experiences has been also studied to gain insights into the image of a destination, (Pan, Maclaurin, & Crotts, 2007; Tussyadiah & Fesenmaier, 2008; Wenger, 2008). Despite these studies' contribution to the current literature on impacts of social media on tourist experiences, the great majority of the literature focuses on the role of social media in the pre-, on-site- and post-visit stage of tourist experiences separately. A holistic conceptual understanding of how tourism experiences are differently and constantly (re)constructed and (re)shaped at the three different stages of tourist experiences remains limited.

This chapter proposes a theoretical conceptual framework that provides a holistic understanding of the role of tourists' engagement with travel blogs in constructing and shaping tourism experiences at the three different stages of tourist experiences. A key theoretical contribution of this chapter is to add to the existing tourist experiences literature by applying a longitudinal approach to understand tourism experiences that are constantly and simultaneously constructed, shaped and packaged at all three different stages of tourist experiences in the context of travel blogs. Findings offer important implications for practical application in the tourism industry, because a better understanding of the experiential aspect of the three stages of tourist experiences (e.g., pre-visit, on-site, and post-visit) is of paramount importance as they can be considered as a foundation for effective tourism marketing and management (Gretzel, Wang, & Fesenmaier, 2012).

THEORETICAL CONSIDERATIONS

Social Media Engagement, Socio-Demographics, and Motivation

Browsing, consuming and active participation are the three levels of engagement used in previous studies to explain people's engagement level with social media (Nonnecke & Preece, 2001; Van Dijck, 2009).

Socio-demographics and motivation are two important factors that influence people's engagement with social media (Bronner & Hoog, 2011; Gretzel, Fesenmaier, Lee, & Tussyadiah, 2011; Wenger, 2008). For example, socio-demographic factors including nationality, culture, gender, education level and age influence the level of tourists' engagement with social media (Gretzel, Kang, & Lee, 2008; Kim, Lehto, & Morrison, 2007). Several studies identify enjoyment, social, and hedonic benefits are the important motivation factors that influences the extent of an individual's engagement in various types of tourism related social media (Bronner & Hoog, 2011; Lin, 2006; Schindler & Bickart, 2004; Wang & Fesenmaier, 2004; Yoo & Gretzel, 2008).

Also, travel blogs, similar to other types of media can be communicated through three main communication modes: information; storytelling, and attraction (Ekström, 2000). Through information, travel blogs represent relevant, interesting and reliable information to appeal to presumptive audiences. Through storytelling, travel blogs convey exciting or dramatic stories to engage those presumptive audiences. Travel blogs also have attraction elements that are presented specifically to fascinate the audience. Travel bloggers therefore use different communication modes in order to communicate their tourism experiences. For instance, they use attraction in remembering/reminiscing about their tourism experiences (Pan et al., 2007) and they construct stories to communicate their personal experiences (Tussyadiah & Fesenmaier, 2008).

THREE STAGES OF TOURIST EXPERIENCE IN THE CONTEXT OF TRAVEL BLOG

From the perspective of tourist behavior (Pearce, 2005), tourist experiences are divisible into three stages; pre-, on-site-, and post-visit. At the early stage of tourist experiences, the use of travel blog helps tourists to learn about potential destination. Tourists engage with various types of information at this stage and that gained information will lead them to construct their own tourism experiences during and after the travel is completed (Mansson, 2011). Assessing other tourists' experiences in travel blogs — that are portrayed in various forms including texts, photos, and videos — enables (potential) tourists to imagine, become inspired and help to narrow down their destination choices (Fotis et al., 2011). The tourism experiences continue to be (re)shaped by technological advancement, as tourists constantly and simultaneously engage with the travel blogs during the trip in real time.

The availability of internet connections at the location and constant use of mobile technologies enables tourists to perform immediate travel tasks such as information searching and the sharing of on-site experiences (Fotis et al., 2011; Gretzel et al., 2011). These technologies also allow the tourists to plan their journey and make decisions while traveling with an immediacy which was not possible previously (Gretzel et al., 2011; Xiang & Gretzel, 2010). Finally, travel blogs continue to play a significant role in the post-visit stage of the tourist experiences. Tourists extend the enjoyment of their visit at the post-visit stage by creating textual, visual, and audio content to help reminisce and to share their experiences with others (Tussyadiah & Fesenmaier, 2009).

CONCEPTUAL FRAMEWORK

The conceptual framework suggests that tourist experiences are an on-going process and continuously changing and altering throughout the different stages of the tourist experience. The key contribution of this conceptual framework is to propose a holistic conceptualization of how tourism experiences are continuously and/or simultaneously (re)constructed, (re)shaped and changed through the pre-visit, on-site and post-visit stage of tourist experiences. A holistic approach is applied as this chapter attempts to understand the process, mechanism and structure between motivations, the levels of travel blog engagement, and tourism experiences construction at the three different stages of tourist experiences. This framework suggests that travel bloggers continuously engage with travel blogs in constructing tourism experiences at the pre-, during, and post-visit stages of tourist experiences and those three stages mutually influence each other to construct and shape tourism experiences.

Also, travel bloggers are assumed to use different types of communication modes and content to construct their tourism experiences in each of the three stages. The level of engagement and motivation not only explains the travel bloggers' behavior and engagement with travel blogs, but also influences the tourism experiences' construction in all three stages. Finally, this chapter examines the influence of the socio-demographic characteristics towards the construction of the tourism experience. The longitudinal approach proposed allows the study to examine the difference or similarity

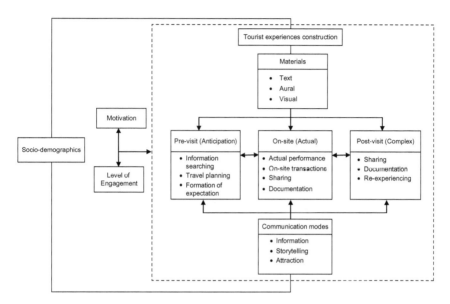

Fig. 1. Conceptual Framework of Socio-Demographics, Motivation, Travel Bloggers Engagement and Tourist Experiences Construction at the Three Stages of Tourist Experiences.

in terms of the tourism experiences construction in the three different stages. Fig. 1 demonstrates a conceptual mapping of the proposed framework of socio-demographics, motivation, travel bloggers engagement and tourist experiences construction at the three stages of tourist experiences.

CONCLUSION AND IMPLICATIONS

While the specific contribution of the study to the relevant tourism literature is discussed, future research is also recommended. First, tourism as a social practice is culturally framed; hence tourism is location dependent. Travel bloggers' activities and engagement with travel blogs and subsequent construction of tourist experiences are related to a certain destination, within the specifics of 'local' values and behavior. Cross-cultural research is required to confirm this. Second, although motivation to engage with social media in terms of tourism experiences construction is explicitly understood, no clear boundaries between motivations of tourism experiences construction and the meaning attached to the experiences are discussed. Further research is recommended to identify a clear separation within those areas to confirm their importance to the constructed tourism experiences.

In conclusion, although prior studies recognize the impact of social media on the tourist experiences, prior studies attempt to examine how tourist anticipation and/or experiences are constructed and shaped only at a specific time period. Tourism experiences are unique and distinctive due to travel bloggers' temporal and spatial ability to create and construct their tourism experiences at any stage, at any moment and in any place/space. The proposed conceptual framework recommends that continuous and simultaneous inter-relationships among these variables are the center of tourist experiences construction in the context of social media in general and in the context of travel blogs specifically.

REFERENCES

Bronner, F., & Hoog, R. D. (2011). Vacationers and eWOM: Who posts, and why, where, and what? *Journal of Travel Research*, *50*(1), 15−26.

Cox, C., Burgess, S., Sellitto, C., & Buultjens, J. (2009). The role of user-generated content in tourists' travel planning behavior. *Journal of Hospitality Marketing & Management*, *18*(8), 743−764.

Ekström, M. (2000). Information, storytelling and attractions: TV journalism in three modes of communication. *Media, Culture & Society*, *22*(4), 465−492.

Fotis, J., Buhalis, D., & Rossides, N. (2011). Social media impact on holiday travel planning: the case of the Russian and the FSU markets. *International Journal of Online Marketing*, *1*(4), 1−14.

Gretzel, U., Fesenmaier, D. R., Lee, Y. J., & Tussyadiah, I. (2011). Narrating travel experiences: The role of new media. In R. Sharpley & P. R. Stone (Eds.), *Tourist experience contemporary perspective* (pp. 170−182). New York, NY: Routledge.

Gretzel, U., Kang, M., & Lee, W. (2008). Differences in consumer-generated media adoption and use: A cross-national perspective. *Journal of Hospitality & Leisure Marketing*, *17*(1−2), 99−120.

Gretzel, U., Wang, Y., & Fesenmaier, D. R. (2012). Travel and tourism. In H. Bidgoli (Ed.), *Handbook of computer networks distributed networks, network planning, control, management and new trends and applications* (pp. 943−961). Hoboken, NJ: John Wiley.

Jun, S. H., Hartwell, H. J., & Buhalis, D. (2012). Impacts of the internet on travel satisfaction and overall life satisfaction. In M. Uysal, R. Perdue, & J. Sirgy (Eds.), *Handbook of tourism and quality-of-life research* (pp. 321−337). Netherlands: Springer.

Kim, D. Y., Lehto, X. Y., & Morrison, A. M. (2007). Gender differences in online travel information search: Implications for marketing communications on the internet. *Tourism Management*, *28*(2), 423–433.

Lin, H.-F. (2006). Understanding behavioral intention to participate in virtual communities. *Cyber Psychology & Behavior, 9*(5), 540–547.

Mansson, M. (2011). Mediatized tourism. *Annals of Tourism Research, 38*(4), 1634–1652.

Nonnecke, B., & Preece, J. (2001). Why lurkers lurk. Paper presented at Seventh Americas Conference on Information Systems, 2–5 August, Boston. Retrieved from skeeter.socs.uoguelph.ca/~nonnecke//research/whylurk.pdf. Accessed on December 11, 2012.

Pan, B., Maclaurin, T., & Crotts, J. C. (2007). Travel blogs and the implications for destination marketing. *Journal of Travel Research, 46*(1), 35–45.

Pearce, P. L. (2005). *Tourist behaviour: Themes and conceptual schemes.* Clevedon: Channel View Books.

Schindler, R. M., & Bickart, B. (2004). Published word of mouth: Referable, consumer-generated information on the Internet. In C. P. Haugtvedt, K. A. Machleit, & R. Yalch (Eds.), *Online consumer psychology: Understanding and influencing consumer behavior in the virtual world* (pp. 35–61). Hillsdale, NJ: Lawrence Erlbaum.

Tussyadiah, I. P., & Fesenmaier, D. R. (2008). Marketing places through first-person stories: An analysis of Pennsylvania roadtripper blog. *Journal of Travel & Tourism Marketing, 25*(3–4), 299–311.

Tussyadiah, I. P., & Fesenmaier, D. R. (2009). Mediating tourist experiences. Access to places via shared videos. *Annals of Tourism Research, 36*(1), 22–40.

Van Dijck, J. (2009). Users like you? Theorizing agency in user-generated content. *Media, Culture, and Society, 31*(1), 41–58.

Wang, Y., & Fesenmaier, D. R. (2004). Towards understanding members' general participation in and active contribution to an online travel community. *Tourism Management, 25*(6), 709–722.

Wenger, A. (2008). Analysis of travel bloggers' characteristics and their communication about Austria as a tourism destination. *Journal of Vacation Marketing, 14*(2), 169–176.

Xiang, Z., & Gretzel, U. (2010). Role of social media in online travel information search. *Tourism Management, 31*(2), 179–188.

Yoo, K. H., & Gretzel, U. (2008). What motivates consumers to write online travel reviews? *Information Technology & Tourism, 10*(4), 283–295.

CHAPTER 11

FACILITATORS AND CONSTRAINTS IN THE PARTICIPATION OF WOMEN IN GOLF

Helena Reis and Antónia Correia

ABSTRACT

This study aims analyzing facilitators/constraints Portuguese women golfers face. The research presents 33 intrapersonal, interpersonal, and structural factors, being supported by a theoretical sampling and data triangulation. The 39 interviews were interpreted by content analysis. Results suggest all participants perceive factors that moderate their participation and highlight dissimilar perceptions by professional and amateur players. Contributions address a manifest heterogeneity: social values prevail even when women are encouraged to join leisure activities. Study limitations derive from the geographical scope restricted to Portugal, yet raising awareness to gender in golf. Stakeholders acknowledge women's low participation; however, this study appears to be the first paper about the subject.

Keywords: Facilitators; constraints; gender; golf; Portugal

Tourists' Perceptions and Assessments
Advances in Culture, Tourism and Hospitality Research, Volume 8, 137–146
Copyright © 2014 by Emerald Group Publishing Limited
All rights of reproduction in any form reserved
ISSN: 1871-3173/doi:10.1108/S1871-317320140000008008

INTRODUCTION

For centuries, golf has been perceived as an elitist sport for older people with a high socioeconomic background: golf was a "man's game" following the pattern of the "for-gentlemen-only" British clubs (Chambers, 1995). Under this influence, it was acceptable for golf clubs to exclude women, not admitting any female members. The British introduced golf around the world and maintained gendered practices. Reis, Correia, and McGinnis (2013) inform, "When the British opened the 1st course, some Portuguese were allowed to play, especially if they had businesses with the British, but the first Portuguese member was only accepted in 1921. It was only after 1932 that women who were close relatives to a member of the club ("still alive or deceased") could eventually become members (Reis et al., 2013). Nonetheless, many women have succeeded in golf and today, 20−25 percent of the golf population in United States, Europe or Australia, are women (EGA, 2012; McGinnis & Gentry, 2006). This study emerged from evidence that Portugal follows this pattern (EGA, 2012; Reis & Correia, 2013).

Considering that more female golfers may contribute to the economic growth of this sector, we found grounds for our research that aim at disclosing the factors that most inhibit or facilitate women's participation. This research relies on the three dimensions of factors (intrapersonal, interpersonal and structural) (Crawford, Jackson, & Godbey, 1991; Godbey, Crawford, & Shen, 2010) acting as constraints/facilitators (Jackson, 2005; Raymore, 2002) to participation. The study comprises 39 interviews with Portuguese female golfers, from champions to "social golfers" without handicap. Our aim is to verify whether these women perceive any facilitators/constraints to their participation and if professional and amateur golfers show different behaviors.

THEORETICAL CONSIDERATIONS

Literature on sports (McGinnis & Gentry, 2006; Reis & Correia, 2013) apply the facilitators/constraints paradigm to deepen the research on leisure and sports participation. Crawford et al. (1991) posit three dimensions of factors: intrapersonal, interpersonal, and structural. The intrapersonal relate to the individual's inner self. The interpersonal examines social interactions and the structural constraints are external factors that inhibit participation, such as social background, socioeconomic status, institutions, infrastructures, race, and gender (Raymore, 2002). This theory was "widely adopted as an important lens through which to view leisure behavior" (Godbey et al., 2010, p. 111) and the authors revisited and assessed their models in 2010, since they have been a reference used in countless leisure research studies.

The 3D factors are assumed to be the main drivers of consumer behavior; thus leading to an understanding of what inhibits women's participation in golf. Reis and Correia (2013) advanced a theoretical model deriving from the literature and life stories of Anglo-American women who excelled in golf in the 19th and 20th centuries. These authors tested the model with six Portuguese professionals and champions having concluded that a number of factors persist throughout the centuries and across nationalities (Reis & Correia, 2013). It is our aim to adopt the aforementioned research to a large sample of women players to assess which factors and to what extent they are perceived as inhibitor/enablers by players with varied levels of golf experience, different life contexts and backgrounds.

METHOD

The study is based on 39 in-depth interviews using a theoretical sampling approach (Glaser & Strauss, 1967; Woodside, MacDonald, & Burford, 2005). This sampling strategy focuses on exploring inhibitors and enablers relating to Portuguese female Professional and Amateur golfers, comprising the profiles based on social status, in accordance with McGinnis, Chun, and McQuillian (2003), since many constraints women experience in sport participation derive from their social condition: age group, marital status and with or without children. The sample comprises different sub-groups: dissimilar golf experience (from the Professional and Amateur champions to women without handicap who are still starting, "social golfers"); *age group* (24 under 40; 15 over 40); *marital status* (21 married; 18 single/ divorced), and *women with* (12) or *without children* (9).

The following presuppositions frame this study. P1: Identify the most important factors that female golfers perceive as facilitators/inhibitors to their participation. P2: Distinguish the most important factors by professional and amateur golfers. P3: Depict the influence of these women's socio-demographic characteristics on their perceptions.

To evaluate the research proposals of this study, the authors relied on Denzin and Lincoln's (2011) suggestion that "qualitative investigators think they can get closer to the actor's perspective through detailed interviewing and observation" (Denzin & Lincoln, 2011, p. 12), which is why we consider qualitative investigation to be the most suitable approach to get a holistic understanding of undisclosed facts. Our research draws on a snowball sampling, to reach participants through "formal and informal networks connections" (Jennings, 2010, p. 140). The interviews were all conducted face-to-face, in Portuguese, duration ranging from 1h30 to 4h30. Interviews were recorded and verbatim transcribed.

The interviewees' verbalizations were interpreted through content analysis (Jennings, 2010), since it provides detailed information that allows interpretation on various levels, according to different contexts. A "theme codebook" (La Pelle, 2004) was created including the three dimensions and the set of 33 factors that had emerged from the literature. This allows counting the number of instances per factor, to know how many women mentioned each factor and which respondent mentioned it. The factors with a higher number of instances are clearly perceived, whilst a lower number of instances indicates that even when women are aware of the relevance of those factors, they do not verbalize them so spontaneously.

FINDINGS

Our sample comprises women from all over Portugal, having recorded 1,272 instances, each corresponding to a sentence/extract. Table 1 includes percentages by factor and interpretative extracts from interviews illustrate the factors with "the voices of the participants."

On the intrapersonal level, personality and motivation emerge as the most significant, conforming with the literature. According to Khan (2011) women's "personality traits rely on being understanding, caring, nurturing, responsible, considerate, sensitive, intuitive, passionate and having the ability to focus on communal goals" (Khan, 2011, p. 107). Regarding motivation, Evans, Jamal, and Foxall (2006) posit that "as positive motivation, people are looking for positive situations, positive mood; pleasure, sensory gratification, intellectual stimulation, social approval and comfort: things that may enrich their lives and are worthwhile to strive for and goals that they want to reach" (Evans et al., 2006, p. 6). Professionals and amateurs with low handicaps show competitive personalities and are motivated to beat men.

Table 1. Dimensions and Factors Illustrated by Excerpts from Interviews.

Dimensions	Percent	Factors	Excerpts From Interviews
Intrapersonal 274 instances	Facilitators 80.6	Personality	I was born to win! I never give up! I love what I do! (Maria, 34, single).
		Motivation	First we start practicing, and then we win a tournament and another one and again, more and more, until one day you represent your country and go abroad … (Lilly, 28, single).
	Constraints 19.34	Lack of motivation	I do not like sports. I tried golf and it is different … but, honestly, I only play because I work here and they [the managers] incentivize us to participate. (Nelly, 39, single).
		Lack of self-esteem	I don't play well, my husband does. (Leila, 61, married, son + daughter).
Interpersonal 481 instances	Facilitators 56.34	Group of friends Social golf	We did everything together and we even had a "special group-suntan" because we spent most of our time on the course, not on the beach. So the sleeves, the shorts, the socks, but above all, the glove, just one hand … It was good; no one made fun of each other because we were all alike. (Rose, 25, single).
		Family incentive	Golf has been in my family for four generations, from my grandfather to my daughter. (Claire, 38, married, one daughter).
	Constraints 43.66	Gender differences	Men buy souvenirs with the course logo or the Masters logos … but ladies like the articles without the logos and they want things to match. (Nelly, 39, single).
		Ethics of care	I didn't want to leave my mother so I didn't go abroad for some years, I was afraid something might happen to her whilst I was away. (Berta, 67, single).
Structural 517 instances	Facilitators 18.2	Good course conduciveness	The courses environment is quite comfortable, not masculinized, this has changed a lot. The clubhouses now are really charming, they are all very elegant. (Jo, 53, married, two children).
		Geo location (near)	When I bought the house, I chose that condominium also because the golf course is within the condominium. (Maggie, a46, divorced, no children).

Table 1.   (*Continued*)

Dimensions	Percent	Factors	Excerpts From Interviews
	Constraints 81.8	Golf institutions course policy/ conduciveness	The female National Team doesn't even have a coach … it is the same as the masculine team, *in his spare time!* (Katie, 24, single).
		Cultural/social attitudes	Many men don't want to play along with women, no matter what their handicap is … it is a cultural prejudice, it is the chauvinistic tradition, independently from the game itself. (Rachel, 31, married, one child).
		Lack of time	Time is a strong problem: it is not the same as using your lunch pause to go to the hairdresser or do some quick shopping. Here you have to change cloths, get equipped, warm up, and then take a shower after the game … it all takes time. (Joana, 47, married, no children).
		Geo location (far)	Now, with my daughter, I end up doing something else, nearer to our home … the beach, for instance. (Candice, 36, married, one child).

On the interpersonal level the strongest facilitator is group of friends followed by family incentive, normally father or husband/boyfriend. The more verbalised constraints are gender differences, meaning physical, psychological, mental or even consumption habits, according to Koc (2004). The ethics of care, engrained in the Portuguese cultural tradition, conforms to the definition of this factor: [women] "provide for the needs of others first (e.g., children, elderly, domestic partner) and neglect their own leisure needs" (Henderson & Allen, 1991, p. 11).

The structural level reveals that these women are very aware of difficulties related to golf institutions/course conduciveness. Effectively, some of the participants belong to the national team and criticize the FPG (Portuguese Golf Federation); cultural/social attitudes can take on many faces, sometimes more subtlety, sometimes openly. For some of our interviewees, lack of time is a real constraint, whilst others state it is "an excuse, you just have to make your options". However, positive course conduciveness is quoted as the more evident facilitator by many women, indicating that a number of the interviewees recognize that golf policies are changing to make courses more women-friendly. Geographic location interferes with female participation in golf, not only for women with children, which is expectable, but also acts as an enabler, showing both sides of the coin. Conversely, professional golfers and women with lower handicap do not find it relevant since they travel around to play.

Comparing Professional and Amateur Golfers

Amateurs' results confirm the verbalization of more facilitators than constraints on both intra- and interpersonal levels. On the structural dimension, the discrepancy is not as accentuated as for the professionals (Table 2).

For the amateur players, motivation has more weight than self-esteem/ competitiveness, which is the main drive for the professionals. Yet lack of motivation is also highly referenced by amateurs and ignored by professionals. The major interpersonal enabler for the amateurs is clearly group

Table 2. Comparing Professional and Amateur Golfers.

Dimensions		Factors	Professionals Percentage	Amateurs Percentage
Intrapersonal	Facilitators	Self-esteem/competitiveness	29.73	18.37
		Personality	29.73	31.29
		Motivation	22.97	34.01
	Constraints	Lack of motivation	–	44.19
Interpersonal	Facilitators	Group of friends/Social golf	32.65	60.81
		Family incentive	32.65	22.97
	Constraints	Ethics of care	19.64	28.57
		Family obligations	3.57	11.69
		Spousal interaction	17.86	5.84
		Gender differences	21.43	38.31
		Professional context/University Studies	21.43	2.6
		Missing social life	12.5	8.10
Structural	Facilitators	Good course conduciveness	–	61.63
		Geo location (near)	–	22.09
	Constraints	Golf institutions and course policy/conduciveness	44.71	43.20
		Cultural/social attitudes	28.24	20.71
		Lack of money	11.76	10.06
		Geo location (far)	5.88	5.62
		Lack of time	2.35	15.09

of friends in comparison to family incentive whilst the professionals value both equally. Amateurs verbalize more family obligations: "household responsibilities are still seen as a woman's 'job' and it is all very time consuming. We never have much free time, with all those family obligations" (Candice, 36, married, one child), whereas professionals find spousal interaction more interfering: "When I coach couples, many husbands tend to 'teach' their wives but they are also just learning ... wives tend to stagnate their evolution and lose interest" (Claire, 38, one daughter). University studies and missing social life are inhibitors visibly less pertinent to amateurs than to professionals. Judith faces a dilemma — studying or playing? She guesses boys would not hesitate: "Boys will easily suspend their studies for a couple of years to play golf, while girls won't", whereas Angela (19, single) faces a choice: "I miss the parties and going out at night with my friends, but I chose to play, so ... ."

On the structural dimension, amateurs find good course conduciveness and geographic location worth highlighting, whilst professionals are more critical about the first whilst the second does not hamper their practice, as they constantly travel. The last main dissimilarity between these two groups is the verbalization of lack of time. Professionals were very incisive declaring that it is a question of organization and priorities, but married amateurs, with children, perceive lack of time as a major limitation.

CONCLUSION AND IMPLICATIONS

Our analysis highlights discrepancies between the two groups (professionals and amateurs): on the intrapersonal level, professionals reveal self-esteem and personality as the main drivers whilst amateurs indicate motivation, which is expectable since professionals are characterized by a strong will and determination to win since motivation may come from external influence (health, open air activity or being with friends). The interpersonal level shows that incentive comes from family for both groups or from group of friends for the amateurs, this being a sign that without the approval of their peer groups some women will quit playing. Women seem to be more dependent on social emulation than any other members of Portuguese society. Surprisingly, even the professionals play mostly because their families/ friends approve of their choice for golf, but some respondents admit that they would interrupt practice to please others (husband/boyfriend, best friends). These findings indicate women's social dependence, proving that the sense of belonging/conformity, determines behaviors, which is according to MacCannell (1976), who posits that conformity refers to the behaviors or attitudes that conform to social norms in strict accordance with peer group membership.

The constraints also vary. Professionals verbalize more spousal interaction, whilst amateurs mention family obligations. Once again, the need for social emulation is present, that is, their families' recognition, making these women postpone leisure pleasures for the sake of others. Professionals face constraints that are stronger for them: balancing golf with university studies and missing socializing with friends. Geographical location (distance home/course) and lack of time are important for amateur married women, especially with children, factors that professionals devaluate since they frequently travel to play in different courses/countries, and consider lack of time a "false constraint" feeling it is more a question of choosing your priorities. When comparing profiles within the amateur group, friends are a great motivator for single women in comparison to married women with children, who do not have much time to socialize. Family obligations are more verbalized by women over 40, maybe due to the burdens imposed on women with families. Many of these women, mainly the single and younger, were incentivized to play by their fathers/family.

The contribution of this study relates to the heterogeneity that is manifest in this cultural background. Overall, social values prevail even when women are encouraged to take part in leisure activities such as golf. Seeing how this heterogeneity plays itself out in different groups, other sports and leisure activities remains a question for future research. Further contributions are expounded on a theoretical level. Expanding the facilitators/constraints perception unveils the factors that influence women to choose a masculine sport. Understanding their behavior provides better awareness of the gender bias that still exists in golf.

By studying strategies top Portuguese female golfers use, we open paths for ways to make golf more appealing to women and for other women to understand how to negotiate their participation irrespective of their desired participation levels and golf experience. Factors of participation found in Portugal conform to the ones advanced by previous research and apply to diverse levels of golf experience (professional, amateur, and social golfers), indicating that these factors are transversal to various nationalities and degrees of involvement. Additional studies are necessary to consider the pertinence of these factors amongst other sports, nationalities and levels of experience a, in a more diversified group of players and within different cultural contexts and sporting activities.

REFERENCES

Chambers, M. (1995). *The unplayable lie: The untold story of women and discrimination in American golf.* New York, NY: Golf Digest.

Crawford, D., Jackson, E., & Godbey, G. (1991). A hierarchical model of leisure constraints. *Leisure Sciences, 13,* 309–320.

Denzin, N., & Lincoln, Y. S. (2011). *The SAGE handbook of qualitative research.* California: Sage.

EGA – European Golf Association. (2012). Retrieved from http://www.ega-golf.ch. Accessed on August 11, 2012.

Evans, M., Jamal, A., & Foxall, G. (2006). *Consumer behavior.* West Sussex: Wiley.

FPG – Portuguese Golf Federation. (2013). Retrieved from www.fpg.pt. Accessed on January 12, 2013.

Glaser, B., & Strauss, A. (1967). *The discovery of grounded theory: Strategies for qualitative research.* London: Wiedenfeld and Nicholson.

Godbey, G., Crawford, D., & Shen, X. (2010). Assessing hierarchical leisure constraints theory after two decades. *Journal of Leisure Research, 42*(1), 111–134.

Henderson, K. A., & Allen, K. (1991). The ethic of care: Leisure possibilities and constraints for women. *Society and Leisure, 14*(1), 97–114.

Jackson, E. (Ed.). (2005). *Constraints to leisure* (pp. 75–88). State College, PA: Venture Publishing Inc.

Jennings, G. (2010). *Tourism research* (2nd ed.). Australia: John Wiley & Sons Australia, Ltd.

Khan, S. (2011). Gendered leisure: Are women more constrained in travel for leisure? *TOURISMOS: An International Multidisciplinary Journal of Tourism, 6*(1), 105–121.

Koc, E. (2004). The role of family members in the family holiday purchase decision-making process. *International Journal of Hospitality & Tourism Administration, 5*(2), 85–102.

La Pelle, N. (2004). Simplifying qualitative data analysis using general purpose software tools. *Field Methods, 16*(1), 85–108.

MacCannell, D. (1976). *The tourist: A new theory of the leisure class.* New York, NY: Schocken Books.

McGinnis, L., Chun, S., & McQuillian, J. (2003). A review of gendered consumption in sport and leisure. *Academy of Marketing Science Review, 5,* 1–24.

McGinnis, L., & Gentry, J. (2006). Getting past the red tees: Constraints women face in golf and strategies to help them stay. *Journal of Sport Management, 20,* 218–247.

Raymore, L. (2002). Facilitators to leisure. *Journal of Leisure Research, 34,* 37–51.

Reis, H., & Correia, A. (2013). Gender asymmetries in golf participation. *Journal of Hospitality Marketing & Management, 22*(1), 67–91.

Reis, H., Correia, A., & McGinnis, L. (2013). Women's strategies to succeed in golf – Portuguese golf professionals – submitted a conference.

Woodside, A., MacDonald, R., & Burford, M. (2005). Holistic case-based modelling of customer's thinking-doing destination choice. In R. March & A. Woodside (Eds.), *Tourism behavior: Travellers' decisions and actions* (pp. 73–111). Wallingford: CABI Publishing.

CHAPTER 12

HOSPITALITY MEANINGS AND CONSEQUENCES AMONG HOTELS EMPLOYEES AND GUESTS

Hamida Skandrani and Mariem Kamoun

ABSTRACT

The purpose of this chapter is to identify hospitality meanings among hotels employees and guests and its consequences on guests' intention. A qualitative approach using in-depth interviews was used for data collection. The study findings reveal that hospitality definitions range from state of mind to service management oriented. Also, hospitality conception seems to have a pentagonal structure revolving around personalization, comfort, relationship guest/host, hospitableness and warm welcoming dimensions. Besides, Mediterranean culture, satisfying and understanding guests' needs appear to influence hospitality perceptions. Cultural sensitivity is a critical skill that may help hospitality providers in coping with guests' cultural differences. Finally, hospitality perceptions may foster behavioral and affective loyalty.

Keywords: Hospitality dimensions; mediterranean culture; cultural sensitivity; loyalty

Tourists' Perceptions and Assessments
Advances in Culture, Tourism and Hospitality Research, Volume 8, 147–156
Copyright © 2014 by Emerald Group Publishing Limited
All rights of reproduction in any form reserved
ISSN: 1871-3173/doi:10.1108/S1871-317320140000008009

· INTRODUCTION

Hospitality has become of a major interest for marketing academicians as well as for practitioners in the hospitality and tourism industry (HTI). Indeed, in the academic sphere, hospitality is widely recognized as another facet of the service industry (Lashley, 2008) that needs better understanding particularly regarding to its meanings, antecedents, and consequences on tourists' decision-making process (Ariffin & Maghzi, 2012; Ariffin et al., 2011; Brotherton & Wood, 2007; Hemmington, 2007; Hepple, Kipps, & Thomson, 1990; King, 1995; Reuland, Choudry, & Fagel, 1985).

From a managerial perspective, the HTI sector is identified as one of the most important and rapidly growing sectors of many national economies (World Travel and Tourism Council, 2011). However, the worldwide growing competition coupled with the many crises the HTI sector has known, threaten seriously the survival of firms operating in this domain, particularly hotels. To overcome these challenges, some firms tried to nurture a culture of hospitality or to take advantage of the hospitality that characterizes a specific culture and to build up guests' loyalty (Chaudhuri & Holbrook, 2001; Hemmington, 2007). Nonetheless, implementing successfully this strategy seems to depend on the extent to which the meanings of hospitality given by employees and guests match up, on how employees manifest their hospitality to their guests and on the consequences on loyalty. Such questionings are particularly important for a country like Tunisia known to be hospitable but also where the HTI sector contributes to the GNP by 14.3% in 2011 and is expected to rise by 5.5% in 2012 and by 3.5% in 2022 (www.wttc.org).

Thus, this study aims at a better understanding of the hospitality meanings among hotels employees and guests. The study also attempts to identify its consequences on guests' intentions and behavior.

THEORETICAL IMPLICATIONS

Hospitality concept seems to lack definitional consensus (Ariffin & Maghzi, 2012; Brotherton & Wood, 2007; Hepple et al., 1990). According to The Canadian Oxford Dictionary (1998), hospitality is the: "friendly and generous reception and entertainment of guests or strangers." For some authors, these definitions of hospitality tend to be relatively broad and unstructured

(Hepple et al., 1990). Others consider the themes of kindness and generosity in making guests or strangers feel welcome, suggest that hospitality is a rather narrow and one-way process without any clear parameters (Brotherton, 1999).

As the interest to hospitality issue has grown, its cultural, historical, and social meanings have provided opportunities to consider its study as distinct from the investigation into the hospitality in the commercial settings. Thus, it is possible to see the field extending beyond commercial hospitality, to hospitality in a social or cultural setting as well as hospitality in the domestic or private setting (Hemmington, 2007; Lashley, 2007, 2008; Thio, 2005).

Four key dimensions of hospitality were identified in hospitality literature. These are: personalization, host–guest relationship, hospitableness and lots of little surprises. Hospitality businesses must focus on the guest experience and develop memorable ones that stimulate all five senses (Hemmington, 2007). They must behave authentically taking responsibility for the experience and creating lots of little surprises (Ariffin & Maghzi, 2012; Brunner-Sperdin, Peters, & Strobl, 2012; Hemmington, 2007). They must respect guests and develop a sense of security and safety. Hospitality organizations that are able to capture this sense of genuine behavior would gain competitive advantage by providing their guests with experiences that are personal, memorable and add value to their lives. They have to treat guests as potential friends (King, 1995; Lashley, 2008).

As competition is growing employees in multiple service sectors and particularly in the hospitality industry are expected to cater guests' needs and to learn continuously about their expectations (Hemmington, 2007; Ro & Wong, 2012). They have to create memorable experiences and to be hospitable. This is likely to encourage guests to return back and to foster not only favorable attitude in behalf them but also "behavioral loyalty" as stated by Hemmington (2007). Besides, loyal customers are more likely to provide strong word-of-mouth or "emotional loyalty" (Dick & Basu, 1994; Hemmington, 2007; Yuksel, Yuksel, & Bilim, 2010).

METHOD

As our study aims to identify the representations of hospitality among guests and hotels employees and to uncover hospitality consequences on guests' intention and behavior, a qualitative approach is deemed more appropriate. Indeed such an approach is recognized to help understanding people and the social and cultural contexts within which they live (Myers, 1997).

To achieve the study objectives, we take into account not only the point of view of hotels employees but also the Tunisian and Foreigner guests. This multi-actors approach offers a better understanding of the hospitality representations among key actors in the Tunisian context, acknowledged to be hospitable. Hotels employees were selected from diverse types of hotels in Tunisia, 9 hotels belong to international hotel chains and 7 hotels belong to national hotel chains, 7 out of 23 hotels are private.

In-depth interviews were carried out with the respondents. A semi-structured interview guide was used and interviews lasted for an average of 30 minutes. Content analysis was performed based on Miles and Huberman (1984) three steps approach: (1) data reduction; (2) data display; and (3) drawing and verifying conclusions.

FINDINGS

Many definitions of hospitality were proposed by the interviewed employees. However, two main categories of definitions emerged: (1) service management oriented definitions and (2) philosophy oriented definitions.

The service management orientated definition has more focus on customer satisfaction, complaint management, reception/welcome, and genuine hospitality. "I can identify hospitality in two words: service provision and customer's satisfaction" (Male, General Manager of a 4-star hotel, 6 years' experience).

The second definition is more philosophy or state of mind oriented in so far as respondents considered the hospitality as a way of thinking and even an art. "Hospitality is an art, tourism is an art, and people who work in the tourism field have to be 'artist'" (Male, receptionist in a 5-star hotel, experience: 13 years).

Noting that the definition that had been most often identified in the literature was economy oriented. To the best of our knowledge no definition presenting hospitality as a service management or state of mind orientation had been suggested in HTI literature.

DIMENSIONS OF HOSPITALITY IN THE HOTEL INDUSTRY

Warm Welcoming

According to our interviewees, warm welcoming seems to be an important dimension of hospitality ($n = 43$). Twenty employees suggested that the most critical part of hospitality is the warm greeting and opening of the door to the guests at the hotel main entrance. In this regard, an employee reported on how he introduces himself to guests upon arrival: "Hello everybody my name is Slim but I am fat boy, I'm going to make your holidays great! I am going to make you happy all your stay. I introduce myself with the animation group and all the staff and we explain for them that we are here to make them happy" (Male, General Manager in a 5-star hotel, experience: 14 years).

The results also show that appreciation tokens such as welcoming drinks or gifts upon checking-in at the reception are considered as means to create surprise and excitement in the hotel hospitality. Ariffin and Maghzi (2012) had already put emphasis on such aspect.

Guest/Host Relationship

The content analysis showed that employees may develop long-term relationships with guests. Indeed, 22 hotels employees (out of 23) stated that they build up long-term relationship especially with loyal guests, and they try to keep in touch with them via letters, emails or Facebook. "It's good to have an intimate relationship between employees and customers. We have friendly relations with our customers, especially by our welcoming, our sympathy and courtesy" (Female, Guest Relations Manager, experience: 13 years).

On the other hand, 30 interviewed guests (out of 34) mentioned that they developed a good relationship with the hotel employees. "Employees are very friendly, very helpful, very friendly … .the staff is very friendly, and we get everything we ask for, they give flowers for the ladies … . The Chief executive officer of the hotel is very friendly" (Female, Irish, repeat visitor).

The findings are, in part, consistent with Hepple et al. (1990) ones. Indeed for these authors the relationship between hosts and guests connotes a sense of ambivalent friendship and hostility.

Personalization

The results of our study show that some employees make personalized welcome by preparing in advance welcome letters according to the nationalities of the guests. Also, remembering names of the guests appears as a personalized treatment. "Basically, I do special and personalized welcome, I know in advance when customers will come, I prepare in advance welcome letters, according to the nationality of the customer" (Female, Guest Relations Manager in a 5-star hotel, experience: 13 years).

In fact, guests seem to highly appreciate such personalized care. Being able to remember the names, nationalities and personal information of guests makes them feel valued and important, and creates a good customer experience. Ariffin and Maghzi (2012) has already shown that personalization is an important dimension of hospitality because it offers a distinct advantage in the hotel industry.

Comfort

Comfort seems to be one of the important tangible aspects of hotel offerings, according to our respondents (guests and hotels employees). This aspect refers especially to the conditions of the guests' rooms. In this line, an accommodation manager (5-star hotel) contended: "the comfort of the rooms and the services in our hotels are the best; there are plasma screens, coffee time service, bottled water is always available, wifi, everything is available" (M, Exp: 6 years). Some authors had already pointed out that hospitality encompasses a blend of tangible and intangible factors (Reuland et al., 1985; Ariffin et al., 2011).

Hospitableness

According to our respondents, hotels employees should be highly hospitable and use emotional intelligence when delivering services to better understand guests and to cater their needs. "We call from time to time our clients when they are in their rooms. I don't wait customers to come to talk about their demands" (Female, Guest Relations Manager in a 5-star hotel, Experience: 13 years).

HOSPITALITY ANTECEDENTS

Our results show that employee hospitable attitude and behavior is identified as the major dimension of hospitableness. Such a hospitable attitude and behavior is deeply rooted in the Tunisian culture but also shaped by an increasingly awareness of guests cultures and by shared norms and values. In this regard, the results revealed that hospitality in the Tunisian context is embedded in the Mediterranean culture and especially in the North African one which receives guests by generosity and warm welcoming. "Generally speaking, people in the Mediterranean are very pleasant and welcoming; such behavior is deeply embedded in our traditions. Kindness and warm welcoming are typical of people in the Mediterranean" (Male, Sales Manager in a 5-star hotel, experience: 20 years).

Such a result offers support to Foster (2007) conclusions. Indeed, this author defines Mediterranean hospitality as a process of receiving foreigners and changing them from strangers to guests. Some marketing scholars had already called for a Mediterranean approach in studying marketing phenomena in Mediterranean countries. According to Cova and Cova (2002) and Cova (2005), this marketing-view should take into account the specificities of the Mediterranean culture.

The interviewed hotel employees also reported that they take into consideration culture differences when they interact with guests. For example, they are very close with some guests and keep some distance with others depending on the guests' nationalities. These findings offer support to some research findings which revealed that cultural sensitivity is an important skill that can help hospitality providers rapidly adapt and cope with culturally different customers (Kriegl, 2000).

HOSPITALITY CONSEQUENCES

Two main consequences of hospitality were identified in the interviewees (employees and guests) discourses: (1) behavioral loyalty and (2) affective loyalty. In fact, the majority of loyal guests seem to be satisfied with the service they have received. In this regard, an Italian businessman had even considered Tunisia as an adoptive country for him. He noted in this regard: "I've been in this hotel since 1988, Tunisia is my adoptive country, I like this hotel and I am satisfied" (Male, repeat visitor).

Besides, our study revealed that loyal and satisfied guests may display two types of interpersonal communication: (1) word-of-mouth and (2) electronic word-of-mouth. This offers support to the influence of interpersonal communication in the THI (Litvin, Goldsmith, & Pan, 2006). Thus, managing word-of-mouth may be a powerful marketing tool that elicits positive effect on guests. As to electronic word-of-mouth, it appears that unsatisfied guests will spread negative feedback which may lead to harmful consequences and a likely downturn in the industry. Thus, hotels need to deal with these problems and try to solve them timely.

CONCLUSION AND IMPLICATIONS

The main objective of this study is to identify hospitality meanings among hotels employees and guests. Also, it aims to identify its subsequent consequences on guests' intentions and behavior. The study offers better insights into the divergences and similarities in hospitality representations among two major actors of the hospitality sector.

Consistent with this objective a qualitative study approach was conducted. Thirty four hotels employees having different professional positions and twenty three guests from different categories of age were interviewed.

Findings with regard to our objectives were very insightful. Indeed, our results allowed classifying hospitality definitions into two classes: philosophy or state of mind oriented definition and service management oriented. Also, the hospitality in the hotel sector may be explained using a five-dimension structure namely personalization, comfort, relationship guest/ host, hospitableness, and warm welcoming.

From a theoretical perspective, this study contributes to the existing literature by offering new insights into hospitality conception by taking into account two major actors of the hospitality industry namely hotels employees and tourists. To the best of our knowledge, previous studies have examined hospitality issue either from the guest's perspective or the employee's perspective, but rarely from both.

Despite the study contributions, some limitations may be addressed. First, the explanatory nature of study inhibits the generalization of the findings to the whole population of employees and guests. This limitation could be overcome in future studies by a quantitative study to investigate into the different relations identified. Second, the hospitality industry comprises other important actors: restaurants, café, travel agencies, and airports. Consequently, future studies are necessary to examine the influence of these actors on hospitality perceptions and meanings. Other studies may examine samples from different countries such as Morocco or/and Turkey. More broadly, studies are also needed to understand what dimensions of hospitality are of utmost importance to the business guests compared to the holiday guests.

REFERENCES

Ariffin, A. A. M., Aziz, N. A., & Maghzi, A. (2011). Understanding novelty-seeking behaviour in meeting tourism: A measurement development approach. *International Review of Business Research Papers, 7*(1), 340–349.

Ariffin, A. A. M., & Maghzi, A. (2012). A preliminary study on customer expectations of hotel hospitality: Influences of personal and hotel factors. *International Journal of Hospitality Management, 31*(1), 191–198.

Barber, K. (Ed.). (1998). *The canadian oxford dictionary.* New York, NY: Oxford University Press.

Brotherton, B. (1999). Towards a definitive view of the nature of hospitality and hospitality management. *International Journal of Contemporary Hospitality Management, 11*(4), 165–173.

Brotherton, B., & Wood, R. C. (2007). *Key themes in hospitality management, the sage handbook of hospitality management* (pp.35–61). London: Sage.

Brunner-Sperdin, A., Peters, M., & Strobl, A. (2012). It is all about the emotional state: Managing tourists' experiences. *International Journal of Hospitality Management, 31*(1), 23–30.

Chaudhuri, A., & Holbrook, M. (2001). The chain of effects from brand trust and brand effect to brand performance: The role of brand loyalty. *Journal of Marketing, 65*(2), 81–93.

Cova, B. (2005). Thinking of marketing in meridian terms. *Marketing Theory, 5*(2), 205–214.

Cova, B., & Cova, V. (2002). Tribal marketing: The tribalization of society and its impact on the conduct of marketing. *European Journal of Marketing, 36*(5–6), 595–620.

Dick, A., & Basu, K. (1994). Customer loyalty: Toward an integrated conceptual framework. *Journal of the Academy of Marketing Science, 22*(2), 99–113.

Foster, J. (2007). Hospitality: The Apostle John, Jacques Derrida, and us. *Reformed Perspectives Magazine, 9*(34), 1–13.

Hemmington, N. (2007). From service to experience: Understanding and defining the hospitality business. *The Service Industries Journal, 27*(6), 747–755.

Hepple, J., Kipps, M., & Thomson, J. (1990). The concept of hospitality and an evaluation of its applicability to the experience of hospital patients. *International Journal of Hospitality Management, 9*(4), 305–317.

King, C. A. (1995). What is hospitality? *International Journal of Hospitality Management, 14*(3–4), 219–234.

Kriegl, U. (2000). International hospitality management: Identifying important skills and effective training. *Cornell Hotel and Restaurant Quarterly, 41*(2), 64–71.

Lashley, C. (2007). Discovering hospitality: Observations from recent research. *International Journal of Culture, Tourism and Hospitality Research, 1*(3), 214–226.

Lashley, C. (2008). Studying hospitality: Insight from social science. *Scandinavia, Journal of Hospitality and Tourism, 8*(1), 69–84.

Litvin, S. W., Goldsmith, R. E., & Pan, B. (2006). Electronic word-of-mouth in hospitality and tourism management. *Journal of Tourism Management, 29*(3), 458–468.

Miles, M. B., & Huberman, A. M. (1984), *Qualitative data analysis*. Thousand Oaks, CA: Sage.

Myers, M. D. (1997). Qualitative research in information systems. *Management Information Systems Quarterly, 21*, 241–242.

Reuland, R., Choudry, J., & Fagel, A. (1985). Research in the field of hospitality. *International Journal of Hospitality Management, 4*(4), 141–146.

Ro, H., & Wong, J. (2012). Customer opportunistic complaints management: A critical incident approach. *International Journal of Hospitality Management, 31*(2), 419–427.

Thio, S. (2005). Understanding hospitality activities: Social, private, and commercial domain. *Journal Manajemen Perhotelan, 1*(1), 1–5.

World Travel and Tourism Council. (2011). *Travel & Tourism 2011*. Retrieved from http://www.wttc.org/site_media/uploads/downloads/traveltourism2011.pdf

Yuksel, A., Yuksel, F., & Bilim, Y. (2010). Destination attachment: Effects on customer satisfaction and cognitive, affective and conative loyalty. *Tourism Management, 31*(2), 274–284.

CHAPTER 13

REFLECTIONS ON DESTINATION POSITIONING ANALYSES AND IDENTIFYING COMPETITORS

Andreas H. Zins

ABSTRACT

This chapter enhances insights into destination image and competitor assessments by extending the research framework of perception-based market segmentation by two perspectives: allowing generating individual sets of competitors and contrasting two stages of travel experience: pre- and after trip. The empirical study is based on two samples of leisure travelers: a mix of international travelers who just finished their trip to Thailand and a group of European travelers interested in visiting Thailand. Against conventional assumptions though supporting more recent findings on destination decision making the majority of travelers did not identify any direct competitor.

Keywords: Competitor; destination image; Asia; Thailand

Tourists' Perceptions and Assessments
Advances in Culture, Tourism and Hospitality Research, Volume 8, 157–165
Copyright © 2014 by Emerald Group Publishing Limited
All rights of reproduction in any form reserved
ISSN: 1871-3173/doi:10.1108/S1871-317320140000008010

INTRODUCTION

Studies on destination images either develop or improve conceptual frameworks and methods applied or use existing approaches to new configurations of destination objects contextual advancements; (for reviews see
Gallarza, Saura, & Garcia, 2002; Pike, 2002, 2007; Stepchenkova & Mills,
2010). This chapter tries to make progress in both directions. On the one
hand, the chapter proposes an innovative procedure on how to collect profile data on individually relevant destination alternatives. On the other
hand, its main objective is the application of the simultaneous segmentation
and positioning analysis of a destination including its competitors. This
technique is called perception-based market segmentation and has been
introduced by Dolnicar, Grabler, and Mazanec in 1999. Dolnicar and
Huybers (2010) illustrate this method for short-break holidays in Australia.

While any type of positioning analysis (e.g., through repertory grid,
MDS or PBMS) is conceived to unveil competitive relationships among
brands or destinations based on perceived similarities these attempts cannot
answer the question of the subjective relevance of alternatives. From consumer behavior modeling we assume that travelers reduce step-by-step the
huge number of objectively available destination options to a small number
of relevant and comparable alternatives. Destinations inside such choice
sets are deemed to compete with each other to a large extent.

To strengthen the relevance of the current application of the PBMS
approach this study tried to deepen the understanding about what travelers
of a particular destination (Thailand in this case) think about other destinations. While the conference paper focused mainly on the PBMS exercise
and its outcome, the current reflection on the conference presentation highlights the insights gained on the competitive position based on the destination selection process.

THEORETICAL CONSIDERATIONS

Several studies deliver evidence that (Decrop & Snelders, 2004; Hyde &
Decrop, 2011; Woodside & Martin, 2008; Zins, 2007) decision making for
leisure trips — particularly for destinations — cannot be assumed to be that
clear-cut staged and linear sequential as many traditional buying behavior
models would propose to be. These insights impact upon our understanding of different categories of alternatives known as different sets: awareness

set, evoked or consideration set, choice or decision set (e.g., Crompton & Ankomah, 1993; Woodside & Lysonski, 1989).

Contingent, sometimes long-lasting personal factors limit and focus the destination selection process. Very particular configurations of these contingent factors may trigger the intention to travel to a specific destination so that the classical information search on and evaluation of alternatives does not take place. A few questions immediately emerge: In what way do destinations compete with each other? How can competitive relationships among destinations be captured and interpreted validly? Who are competitors in a multi-destination trip?

The preparatory stage of the study into perceptions-based market segments (PBMS) of travelers to Thailand envisaged to identify individually highly relevant alternative destinations to Thailand. The consecutive measurement of image perceptions should be based on individually defined competitors to Thailand.

Two directions of analyses are taken into consideration. First, differences between travelers who already spent their holidays at the destination and those who are preparing a trip to this destination. Second, a comparison between travelers with different starting configurations for their destination choice: (a) those planning a multi-destination trip, (b) those planning a single-destination trip with a choice set of one alternative only, and (c) those planning a single-destination trip with a larger choice set.

METHOD

A high proportion of destination image studies consider only one destination (one image object only). To compare several destinations or brand objects usually a set of pre-defined alternatives is prepared and later used for the measurement exercise. In order to select only relevant alternative destinations past studies and/or destination management strategies are reviewed. The current study took eight destinations as identified by the Tourism Authority Thailand (TAT) as the most immediate competitors. In addition to that, respondents were invited to add more destination names if they could not find their preferred countries on the given list for answering the particular question. Hence, the analysis will allow a comparison of response densities for pre-defined and subjectively relevant answer categories and enables the usage of individual sets of competitors instead of a pre-defined list of destinations.

To differentiate between different a priori configurations that travelers were subject to when deciding to travel to Thailand the following sequence of questions was applied (see Fig. 1): Prospective travelers to Thailand were identified when visiting the official website of the TAT. To make sure that these respondents strongly intend to visit Thailand a filter question was applied. Only those respondents who were quite sure about the Thailand (94%) or those who were not entirely sure about the final destination (6%) qualified to participate. This sample and the second one with current travelers to Thailand were asked if they this particular trip is a single-destination or a multiple-destination trip. Multiple-destination travelers were treated separately since the question about alternative destinations can be interpreted as complementary destinations and not exclusively as competing ones.

Single-destination travelers were asked if they considered other destinations as alternatives or not. If yes ("flexible travelers"), destinations ticked and/or enumerated in this question can be interpreted as consideration or choice set. For those travelers indicating that there is/was no alternative to be considered ("focused travelers") it is difficult to describe and qualify the relationship with the target destination and with any other. First, it was asked to give reasons why no other destination was considered and second, a projective question was raised about any recommended destination that could be seen as an alternative to Thailand. Differences between destination ranks from recommendations of "focused travelers" and considerations of "flexible travelers" are not expected to be very large. Whereas alternatives listed by single-destination and multiple-destination travelers are expected to deviate more since the latter is supposed to describe more complementary than competitive relationships.

Finally, all respondents were asked about their past destination choice behavior and their travel intentions for the next three years. Past destination choice and a destination preference ranking built upon this past behavior can be recognized as the past or realized competitiveness among destinations. Similarly, the intention to visit a destination within the next three years reflects somehow the attractiveness of the destinations in mind. For both questions, respondents could add countries at their own discretion.

Current travelers to Thailand were invited at major airports (Bangkok, Chiang Mai, Phuket) in Thailand when they left the country after their holiday (February to April 2010). At Chiang Mai airport, mainly face-to-face interviews were conducted. Travelers at the other airports were invited orally and by letters to participate in this survey through the means of an

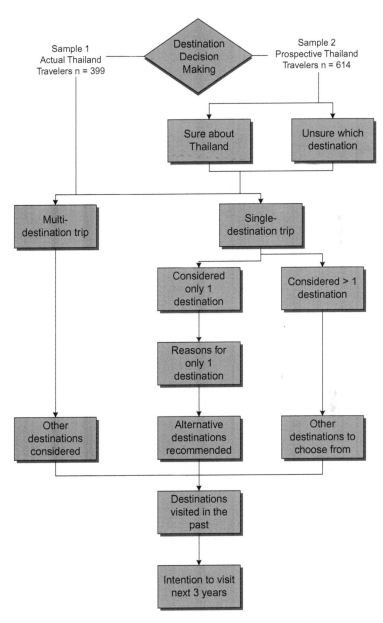

Fig. 1. Flow Chart of Destination Choice Questionnaire Section

online questionnaire. The majority of respondents are in the age bracket between 30 and 39 years. 55% of respondents are male and 45% are female. 61% of the respondents came from European countries, 12% from English speaking overseas countries, 11% from Asian countries, and 16% from other regions. Within Europe some nationalities show a higher frequency: Finnish (10%), British (9%), Swedish (9%), and German (6%). Respondents in general are well educated with 45% having a bachelor and 21% a master or even higher degree. The sample size comprises 319 questionnaires.

Prospective travelers to Thailand were recruited at the official website of the Tourism Authority Thailand in Germany. A special link directed interested website visitors to the online questionnaire similar to that used for the Thailand travelers. From March to the first week of September 2010 a total number of 614 questionnaires were gathered. The average age is slightly higher than that of the first sample with a large proportion of travelers between 40 and 59 years. 60% of the respondents are male. The majority of 80% indicated German nationality, 7% stated Austrian and 9% Swiss nationality. 36% had a bachelor or higher academic degree.

FINDINGS

Overall, the two samples differ by nationality, age and, of course, by the time reference with respect to the trip to Thailand. Sample 2 respondents (prospective travelers) show a tendency toward a higher response density: (a) fewer empty cells (first row of Table 1) and (b) more alternative destinations elicited (second row of Table 1). Using a pre-defined list of alternative destinations covers about 80% of options that have been considered explicitly or implicitly when preparing this trip to Thailand.

Almost one quarter of all respondents planned for a multi-destination trip. In this case, the information about alternative destinations (Table 1, first column of each sample) is indicative for complementary spots to be visited. The frequencies of country names are relatively similar for both samples except for a significantly higher count for India for sample 1 and the Maldives for sample 2.

The majority of travelers (around 60%) reported that they had only one destination in mind (Thailand) when planning the trip (no significant differences between actual and prospective travelers). Among a list of reasons (generated from open-ended interviews with travelers at Phuket

Table 1. Implicit and Explicit Competitors to Thailand as a Travel Destination.

	Sample 1: Actual Thailand Traveler					Sample 2: Prospective Thailand Traveler				
	Multi-Destination	Focused Traveler	Flexible Traveler	Past Visits	Intended Visits	Multi-Destination	Focused Traveler	Flexible Traveler	Past Visits	Intended Visits
No alternatives given	34%	53%	2%	–	–	8%	13%	0%	–	–
N =	41	115	106	277	342	119	313	129	482	593
Average number of destinations	1.9	1.8	1.3	1.4	1.6	2.1	2.3	2.0	1.9	2.1
Share of responses based on pre-defined destinations*	81%	85%	83%	–	–	69%	90%	82%	–	–
Thailand	–	–	–	78%	83%	–	–	–	87%	95%
Bali*	37%	35%	9%	9%	14%	38%	48%	17%	20%	19%
Malaysia*	17%	24%	13%	9%	10%	21%	28%	17%	14%	12%
Vietnam*	34%	24%	26%	10%	11%	32%	42%	26%	10%	20%
Maldives*	10%	21%	6%	4%	7%	20%	25%	5%	7%	8%
Laos*	10%	17%	20%	7%	9%	7%	14%	33%	6%	11%
Singapore*	12%	16%	10%	8%	8%	9%	25%	23%	13%	10%
Cambodia*	7%	14%	15%	2%	8%	13%	17%	36%	8%	13%
India*	27%	4%	6%	4%	5%	2%	5%	8%	2%	4%
Myanmar	4%	0%	4%	1%	2%	7%	2%	7%	2%	2%

Note: *Signficant differences across traveler segments (first three columns of Sample 1 and Sample 2).

International Airport) why no other alternative was considered, 61% checked "because they have been to Thailand before and liked it much," 40% "because it is their dream destination," 32% "because of Thailand's positive reputation," and 28% "because friends recommended to them." Other reasons (14%) are mainly based on family ties and prior work experiences. 53% of the actual travelers did not elicit another country as a recommended alternative to Thailand. This proportion is as low as 13% for those still in the planning phase. As could be expected those "flexible" travelers considering more destinations are more inclined to elicit some alternatives. However, the average number of considered alternatives does not differ much for travelers in the planning stage while it is much lower for "flexible" travelers who are looking back to their planning phase.

The structure of considered versus recommended destination alternatives differs a lot. For actual travelers Bali/Indonesia appears on top of the recommendations as an alternative whereas Vietnam is mentioned most often by "flexible" travelers followed by Laos. In contrast, prospective travelers would recommend Bali/Indonesia must followed by Vietnam. "Flexible" travelers considering more options from the very beginning elicit Bali/Indonesia and Vietnam most frequently followed by Malaysia, Singapore, and the Maldives.

CONCLUSION AND IMPLICATIONS

Using a pre-determined set of destinations for destination image measurement studies entails a remarkable risk of reduced validity. Only a small share of 15% of actual and prospective travelers reported to choose among a smaller (consideration or choice) set of alternatives. On average, only one to two other destinations are elicited. The majority (60%) of travelers are focused to only one destination (Thailand) without considering any alternative for various reasons. Reputation is not listed on top in this context. The different mind-set of these focused travelers is confirmed by the fact that a substantial share of respondents could not give any other country name as a recommended alternative to Thailand. Asking for such recommendations was considered to be a close proxy for implicit competitors. However, the frequencies of recommended and those of considered alternatives differ too much as to assume that these reflections have the same conceptual meaning. Differences, though, can be also attributed to the different reference point: this particular trip with all the individual contingent factors behind versus the general recommendation and comparison detached from a specific context.

Similarly, past and future destination visits represent other dimensions of competitive relationships among destinations. For both samples, no congruence between past visitation and intended visitation patterns on the one hand and the particular consideration set configurations on the other hand could be detected.

Finally, the current experiment of allowing individually different objects/destinations helped to assess the degree of distortion when working with a fixed list of image objects. In this case example respondents could choose from a list of eight country names while being able to (a) ignore all of these and/or (b) add individually relevant ones. Overall, about 85% of the chosen destinations were picked from the presented list while about 15% were added individually. This can be seen as minor, yet, could lead to the ignorance of smaller competitors or market segments.

REFERENCES

Crompton, J. L., & Ankomah, P. K. (1993). Choice set propositions in destination decisions. *Annals of Tourism Research, 20*(3), 461–476.

Decrop, A., & Snelders, D. (2004). Planning the summer vacations: An adaptable process. *Annals of Tourism Research, 31*(4), 1008–1030.

Dolnicar, S., Grabler, K., & Mazanec, J. A. (1999). Analysing destination images: A perceptual charting approach. *Journal of Travel & Tourism Marketing, 8*(4), 43–57.

Dolnicar, S., & Huybers, T. (2010). Different tourists − Different perceptions of different cities. In J. A. Mazanec, & K. Wöber (Eds.), *Analysing international city tourism* (pp. 127–146). Wien: Springer.

Gallarza, M. G., Saura, I. G., & Garcia, H. C. (2002). Destination image. Toward a conceptual framework. *Annals of Tourism Research, 29*(1), 56–78.

Hyde, K. H., & Decrop, A. (2011). New perspectives on vacation decision making. *International Journal of Culture, Tourism and Hospitality Research, 5*(2), 103–111.

Pike, S. (2002). Destination image analysis − A review of 142 papers from 1973 to 2000. *Tourism Management, 23*, 541–549.

Pike, S. (2007). Destination image literature 2001 to 2007. *Acta Turistica, 19*(2), 107–125.

Stepchenkova, S., & Mills, J. (2010). Destination image: A meta-analysis of 2000–2007 research. *Journal of Hospitality Marketing and Management, 19*(6), 575–609.

Woodside, A., & Lysonski, S. (1989). A general model of traveler destination choice. *Journal of Travel Research, 27*(4), 8–14.

Woodside, A., & Martin, D. (2008). Applying ecological systems and micro-tipping point theory for understanding tourists' leisure destination behavior. *Journal of Travel Research, 47*(August), 14–24.

Zins, A. H. (2007). Exploring travel information search behaviour beyond common frontiers. *International Journal of Information Technology & Tourism, 9*(3–4), 149–164.